THE KEEPER OF ME

The Keeper of Me

NELLIE ANITA WOSU

THE KEEPER OF ME

THE KEEPER OF ME

©2012 by
NELLIE ANITA WOSU

Cover Design by: Angela J. Wesley of ALEGNA MEDIA DESIGNS
[www.alegnamediadesigns.com]

Author photo by: Moyeh Moye – [www.profileartistmoye.com]

Library of Congress Cataloging-in-Publication Data

Wosu, Nellie Anita.
    The Keeper of Me.

ISBN-13: 978-0615740386
ISBN-10: 0615740383

We hope you enjoy this book from Gatmoon Publishing. Our goal is to provide high-quality, thought-provoking books and products that connect truth to your real needs and challenges.

Gatmoon Publishing
P.O. Box 1244
Concord, NC 28026

THE KEEPER OF ME

ISBN-13: 978-0615740386
ISBN-10: 0615740383

DEDICATION

This book is dedicated to three of the most important women in my life:

My mother, the late Fernell J. Gatlin, who instilled in me all that she knew of faith and how one was to become an individual who was after God's own heart by always remembering the Golden Rule and loving one and all unconditionally, and to always and in all ways, forgive the self and all others.

Another is my mentor and Spiritual Mother, the late Evangelist Johnnie Mae Moody. She instilled in me what it means to *"Live by Faith"*. Evangelist Moody is to me what air is to life; absolutely essential and totally relevant.

The other, is my daughter, Summer Chiani Wosu. Summer, who is beyond definition, is an amazing young woman, who is continually evolving into her greater self. As she journeys through self-examination and self-discovery, she is mastering what it means to be always true to thine own self. As always, I am most proud of her and continually wish that I had had a friend like her when I was growing up…but then again, I've been granted that, too, for I am still growing up! Love you BIG Sum!

As a person who believes in speaking truth about what matters to the heart, I would be remiss, if I didn't unequivocally state that there is one man that stands apart, far and wide from all others. That man is Nathaniel Pernell Johnson; he has always been my best friend from the time we met more than 22 years ago. Pernell is an enigma; he is truly an individual beyond compare. Pernell moves to his own unique beat. He's never out of sync with his timing and he constantly gives me good reason to look to my Lord for guidance, understanding and truth in matters of the heart. He is the one that challenges me to breathe and rethink what it means to love your best friend. Nathaniel Pernell Johnson is my husband, a gift that arrived at the most unusual and unexpected time in my life, but one that I always hoped for.

I love you BIG Mr. Pernell Bear!

CONTENTS

ACKNOWLEDGMENTS

It has been said that if you want to know about a person, then you should look to the people in their lives. It is those people who you see when you look at me. I am representation of all of the vast encounters that I've had throughout my life. Even if the encounter was but a brief moment in time your presence was felt and the impact was essential to my becoming. Whether you challenged me or embraced me, it was for my good and I thank you for being an integral part of the development of Nellie Anita!

Thank you Zenobia L. Nelson, for your time, consideration and well wishes by assisting me with this labor of love.

Thanks to my Sister-in-Christ, Karen Gronli, your words of inspired truth were as morning dew.

The number of people to acknowledge is too great to be listed here. However, there are certain people that I love deeply and they are like breath to me. It matters not the length of time that I have known them, it comes down to the point of our hearts being in sync with one another. Those individuals are:

Karen A. Groves, childhood friends for life. We've bathed together, we've laughed and cried together; we've loved together; we've been distant together; we came together in matters concerning our hearts and the hearts of those we love.

Adriane E. Rambert, my essential friend and confidant concerning ALL matters of my heart; a woman of deep understanding of life and its many twists in love. Thank you for being a healing balm of love and compassion before, during and in the many seasons of my new life. Your presence is a gift from God.

Denise Cardozo, my long-time friend and former co-worker. When we met, we were very young women, married with children and taking Wall Street by storm. Denise was one of the first persons that I spoke with regarding my decision to have the procedure. Then, as in always, Denise provided heartfelt support and love.

Linda Pyatt, Thelma Chavis, Christine Cooper, Lillian Thomas and Valerie D. Merritt, these women have always been special to me in sharing their life and love while becoming true foundational blessings in my life.

And, my cousins: Rosa M. Carpenter, Tracy Lynn Romans, Juanita Poole, I love you; we are always family on any given day, what a blessing!

There is a family here in North Carolina, the Williams Family, Cookie & Donald Williams, and their children and entire family have gone the extra distance to have me as an honorary member of their family! I am thankful to have them in my life sharing their lives and special family moments with me!

To the ladies of North Carolina! You guys have made the difference in my new life. Your impact is without question, a blessing beyond description. Each of you brings your own splendid colorful essence of joy in my life. You are all lovely, especially:

LaShelle Foster, the foundation to my being here in this relevant time. Barri Spratt, the one who has seen His work in me.

And, Minister Patricia Sanders, one who loves unconditionally and who from afar has the ability to help me see clearly.

Often times, when you arrive in a new place and meet certain individuals, you know instinctively that they are blessed of God and your lives will be a testament of what Jesus Christ does for those who diligently seek Him. To that end, I am thankful for the life of Latarcha Bennett, who is my Spiritual Daughter. She and her husband and children have re-defined the term family. The same is to be likened to Karen Minott who is truly the definition of "God Sent".

Zenobia Nelson and LeVannah Forrest help to add joy to the endeavor of living beyond the bounds of what survey says.

And, to one who has to be (without question) my sister at some time in our lives, Renate A. Moore; a person who I can always count on to be totally real with me and who has the absolute ability to accept me for who I am in any season. Renate has been the continual voice to my getting this labor of love completed, so your journey will be greatly enhanced. LadyRen, I am thankful for you and your family's friendship and love in my life.

Foundations are always the beginning of what is to

become. A solid foundation is essential to establishing the work of the Lord in matters of the heart. With that truth, I must thank and praise God, the Lord and the head of my heart, and my Church Family, the members of First Missionary Baptist Church, Concord, NC, who are an essential part of my continuing working for His glory.

My Pastor and Mentor, Herb Rhedrick Jr., and his lovely wife and my friend, First Lady Gail Rhedrick, who are an answered prayer. Thank you for all you do to encourage me to "Trust God more and myself less." I thank God for you.

I would be totally remiss if I didn't mention the angels who have cared for me prior to, during and after the procedure. These professionals continue to keep me well in mind, body and spirit. It is imperative to have a team of health care professionals who care about you first as a person, while being cognizant of what your concerns are as a patient. The professionals noted below have always placed me, Nellie Anita, first, and I believe that has been an integral component to my growing wellness in every aspect of my health agenda. Sincere thanks to:

The New Jersey Medical Team
Mark Zucker, MD, JD
Laura Adams, RN
Jesus Casida, PhD, APN-C, CCRN-CSC
Newark Beth Israel Medical Center – Cardiology Heart
Failure Treatment & Transplant Center

The North Carolina Medical Team
Paul T. Campbell, MD
Bridget S. Bongaard, MD
Malia Kizer, MA, LPC, NCC
Virginia Adams, RN, BSN, FCN
Carolinas Medical Center-NorthEast
Sanger Heart & Vascular Institute

And, then of course, there is that one special Person that I certainly don't want to overlook - and that person is you! Yes, you, the one who holds this book in your hands reading, sharing and growing from my experience of matters of the heart ... from a mind, body, spirit perspective!

I love you most of all for you are "me" – redefined, growing in love, always pleasing your heavenly Creator by your growing faith and trust in Him ... always in all ways!

"Nellie Wosu is one of the most remarkable women I have ever known. She has faced and overcome challenges in her life through sheer determination, faith and a contagious smile. Her heart disease has not defined her but rather defined her purpose. It has been a pleasure to share in her care over these past 10 years. Nellie is truly an inspiration to me and it is a pleasure knowing such a dynamic lady. I wish her health, success and happiness always."
Laura Adams, RN

But He knows the way that I take;
When He has tested me, I shall come forth as gold.
My foot has held fast to His steps;
I have kept His way and not turned aside.
I have not departed from the commandment of His lips;
I have treasured the words of His mouth
More than my necessary food.

Job 23:10-12

For He is...

The Keeper of Me

"The Keeper of Me" is a story that speaks about the heart from a mind, body, spirit perspective in regards to the healing of both the physical and spiritual heart, mine in particular.

This is a story of my journey with heart disease.

My hope is that this story will inspire you to consider why your heart matters and to always remember to guard it - in all diligence!

Out of the abundance of the heart, the mouth speaks.

In all sincerity and love...
~Nellie Anita!

1 WHEN DID THE END BEGIN

You will keep him in perfect peace, Whose mind is stayed on You, Because he trusts in You. Isaiah 26:3

Long before something manifests itself for us to see, acknowledge and accept, (if we ever do accept it - see it or even and acknowledge it), I believe that that something had already been ordained in our lives before the foundations of the world. And, I also believe, how we maneuver in that truth of designed circumstances, our outcome in navigating through those circumstances, has already, too, been written.

Such would be the case for the myriad of years in which I lived my life; until I came upon a series of subtle changes that would completely change and redefine me beyond anything I would have ever considered. These changes took me to a new level of life and living that I could not have known or recognized as being my life.

My mom used to say the Lord works in mysterious ways His wonders to perform. I pondered what she meant about that at different stages in my life; sometimes more than other times, but lately, this saying kept creeping up in my thoughts. She was always sending some type of message to me...since her transition to new life. Realizing that I needed to pay attention to my thoughts, I shook my head again, not being able to shake that thought. Mommy, what are you telling me? Frustrated, I would shrug off the thought and resume the routine.

I continued to hear *"Listen to your thoughts"* in my mind. What are you saying to yourself? I couldn't hear anything quite frankly.

Just another day as any other day, like the day before, like the week before, like the month before, like the year before, and also like all of the years before that…I sat in my usual seat on the various forms of transportation that would take me to work…the bus in Jersey City, waiting for the LOCAL EXPRESS, the PATH Trains from Jersey City to New York City, and the NYC Subway to work…and ultimately driving my two size 9s better known as "ten toe turbo" to get me to work.

My life consisted of getting up, and going to work, getting to work, and working, going all over the globe, while never leaving my seat. I grew in responsibility and capability. Learning from situations that could have toppled an organization, I was able to once again, help to save the day.

I sure did, did it daily…for a very long time, long enough to no longer hear my own thoughts. I became consumed with my work. I worked practically around the clock. I had two jobs. One full time 40 hours a week job in New York City and a part-time job in New Jersey at about 25 hours per week.

Who was I? I was a Network Tech working in a Fortune 100 Corporation in New York, monitoring the corporation's network, helping to establish a global Help Desk environment in the Corporate Headquarters. One of my responsibilities was to make certain that the critical mail system moved without any disruption or realized interruption. My eyes were constantly peeled for sluggishness in the email system as it went throughout the entire global network for this HUGE behemoth of an entity. Global baby, I was totally global, sitting in my chair in my own office looking out at Park Avenue. I loved my job! I had a reasonable portion of autonomy and a growing spear of influence and a not so small degree of authority. I enjoyed most of my co-workers. We had fun. I was the Lotus Notes guru. Application Development was my game. I was the only person on the team who had that expertise. I was hired because I was a Notes Administrator and was headed on my way to certification in Lotus Notes Apps Development and beyond.

I was also one of the more "seasoned" Techies in the effort. That meant I was the old chick. I was "Mommy," the other Techies lived with their Mommy and Daddy.

There were a few other guys who were my age, but in the corporate realm as a guy matures in age, he gets a certain degree of status. For a woman, you're about to become a relic. At least that was the way it was then. Here we are in the mid to late 90s and I'm beginning to really have a handle on my career. How fortunate was this? My kid was entering Boarding School in the Northeast. My daughter was a true maverick, when it came to Math & Science. She ate up Math & Science just like the Honey Nut Cheerios we so loved to enjoy over our late night conversations on the weekend which were filled with laughter and music as we enjoyed living life with burgeoning financial stability. Had we arrived? Perhaps, but I wasn't certain, I would in fact become quite uncertain of that arrival in a moment or so however, that wasn't evident in those moments. So again, I asked the question, had we arrived? Hmmm, well, maybe so, I thought to myself when I would ponder whether we had actually arrived. What did all of this mean? What does arrival look like for individuals such as us? Surely certain people, when they arrive, have a certain type of distinction. Our arrival seemed to be quiet. Mommy always said to be humble. The question that loomed in my head was if we had in fact arrived, where were we? I didn't have a clue other than the fact that I seemed to have an unending grin on my face, one that made the Kool-Aid guy look like he was frowning.

Money covers up many things within your person, I later would come to realize. Having financial stability as a single parent was always looming in my mind. Wanting to be able to provide for your family is essential and honorable; however, actually providing for your family is sublime. So I was in a blissful state; I was handling my business (which was primarily my daughter). Taking care of our household. I paid my tithes and offerings with all zeal. I was even able to provide for many of our desires too.

Providing for your family is something that any parent would want to be able to do for their families and themselves. It's essential that people be able to handle their affairs, consistently with the funds that they've earned themselves.

First things first, let's not put the cart before the horse. How often I pondered when will this end? My body was tired. Here I was in my late 30s and I had already worked more than half my life. I started working at 15 years old. Finally, I had the career that I had always desired. Technology was truly my game! I loved Tech - the fast pace, being in New York City, what?! The constant change challenged and developed me. I was becoming Corporate America. I cut my teeth in New York. From the time I was 18 years old, I was exposed to big business and big ideas. I've worked with some of the biggest names on Wall Street within Brokerage and Investment Banking. I was on a first name basis with people who were game changers (before that phrase became a phrase); being invited to country clubs and lush mansions for the weekend, staying in 5-star hotels; you name it, it was heady at best.

I knew from experience how things were to be handled in the standard corporate manner; even from a Black perspective, a girl from the hood with obviously no hood in her. Dispelling the myth was my game! I had a view of the lives of the powerful and saw how that power impacted everyone. I stood by learning and was taking it all in. Why was I here to hear, and what was I to do with all of this knowledge? I pondered again, but still no answer. Was this the beginning of my end?'

2 THE BODY IS SPEAKING

Right about this time, I started to feel funny inside. Having lunch with my friend Adriane, I used to tell her that something was wrong inside of me. She being a medical professional, would ask me what I was experiencing. I couldn't quite define the feeling. I knew something was slipping away from me from the inside.

I had always been one to make certain that I did all of my annual medical check-ups without fail. I knew the importance of preventative care. While I didn't always go to the gym, I was physically active in my favorite pastime, dancing! I love, love, love to dance! Dancing was my thing. There would come a time when I could barely breathe and move at the same time let alone dance. That time had begun to show itself by approaching very ominously, stealth and deadly, as an undercover invader.

Time for my quarterly visit to my Internist, I tell her about the changes inside of me. She listens intently. Does the routine blood works. I return once again and everything shows up fine. I got a good report. Here take some vitamins. Eat more fresh vegetables, get out in the air and circulate, and stop working so much! Yep okay. I'll try it. So we gab about fashion and fragrance. Right!

Showering began to be a difficult task. Something is wrong with my legs. They feel rubbery like they can't hold me up. I'm even more tired now. What is really going on? Walking is becoming a chore. Dancing is a bore. Yeah, now I know something is really wrong. When James Brown's music is playing and I sit still, something has definitely gone awry. It's good to know who you are and who you're not in all seasons.

The journey that I had traversed by this time had become a very tedious and twisted saga. When I thought I had cleared one summit, and would go onto the next, I was plummeted into the depths of the abyss without warning. Now my health had become an issue. Hadn't I always kept tabs on my health? Yes, I had, more than would be expected. I always wanted to be completely well.

By the Summer of 1999, my health began to play real games with me, games that were not the least bit funny. These were tricky games. They would cause me to lose my breath and grow weak for no reason, seemingly. Before, I got that ultimate position I had this other job with another huge corporate giant.

Summer, Pernell and I visited with Aunt Cue and Uncle Fred in Concord, for the Fourth of July that summer, we flew down. It was as hot as hades in my aunt and uncle's house! I had to get out of there and go buy them an air-conditioner. I wasn't able to breathe for some reason.

We cut the visit short as I couldn't maintain my strength. It was just too hot. I needed to be back at home. Where according to Sum and Pernell I would become "Chilly Willie". I had taken to having to have the air-conditioner on max high with the fan blowing on me at full capacity for some reason. Without this, I couldn't breathe too well.

Here comes the Invader!

Like a thief in the night, the Invader slammed me. Tired beyond words, more tired than I had ever felt in my life, it happened. One Friday evening after being out with the crew, Summer & Pernell, I went to lie down on my bed, my legs felt funny. I sat on the foot of the bed and a sensation hit me in waves. Strange sensation I thought to myself. I'm going to have to do better. I'm just too tired. I need to rest a bit more working too hard. I must have been either too quiet or gone for too long. Pernell came and said something to me. I responded somehow. He called my name. I was riding that funny sensation wave. Neat, he called, what's wrong? I was dazed. "nothing" I heard myself say. Neat, Neat! Neat what's wrong? 'nothing.' Neat you want to go to the hospital? 'no.' I'm okay I managed to say. By that time, here comes Summer. Mommy what's wrong? You okay? Yes babe, I'm okay. "You sound funny" she said. I tried to make a joke, you know I always sound funny Button, I'm okay.

Pernell still looking at me, "Neat let me take you to the hospital." No, I'm good, I'll be okay. Just take me to the doctor in the morning, okay?" He reluctantly agreed and said I should get ready for bed and I should get up. I said okay I would. The truth was that I couldn't get up. Someone had put a slab of lead on my chest that was invisible.

Somehow at some point, I managed to get up and get ready for bed. I sat up in bed all night at a 90 degree angle with that fan blowing directly on me, and the air up to Artic proportions so I could breathe.

Morning finally comes and I take my shower, but there it began to happen again. The Invader came again and threw me up against the walls of the shower. Gasping for breath I nearly passed out. I got out and dressed at a snail's pace. Pernell took me to the doctor. I went in and told her what was going on. She looked at me long and hard. Nellie, take your top off and get up on the table. She got out the stethoscope did her thing for too long. The doctor rolls out the EKG machine. I asked her about her tech. Why wasn't the Tech doing the EKG? The doctor said she wanted to take care of me. She hooked me up…the test began to roll. She read the strip…her face changed colors. She looked at me and swallowed I could tell. Nellie get up she said in a type of hushed voice. Then she said you're going to the ER now in a firm tone. I said flat out 'Oh no I'm NOT!" She said, Nellie, you're going to the ER NOW!!! I said again, No I'm NOT. Nellie. What? You must go to the ER Now. I can't Dr. How long will I be there? I don't know she said? Then I know I can't go. I have a minor child at home. I can't just go to the ER. And, Pernell, will have to go back to work tomorrow.

This went on back and forth for a while. Finally, I got her to see my side. She wrote a prescription and told me to get it filled immediately and go to the hospital after I handle the affairs concerning my daughter.

Long story short, I entered into the hospital the next morning round 'bout midnight or so on Sunday morning. It had taken that long to secure an appropriate housing situation for my daughter to be comfortable in and safely cared for and for me to be content and secure that Summer was going to be alright without my presence for an undetermined amount of time.

3 THE PROMOTION

Deuteronomy 8:18
"And you shall remember the LORD your God, for it is He who gives you power to get wealth, that He may establish His covenant which He swore to your fathers, as it is this day.

An opportunity presented itself for me to obtain a new second job! I wouldn't need to work every day at the part-time job. I was blessed with a part-time job that I only needed to work on weekends. The thing was that I had to work a twelve hour day on Friday night and Saturday night. Hmmm…yet again. So, yes, you calculated it correctly on Friday's I was up at about 6:00 am or just before, to leave by 7:30 am, to be at work at 9:00 am, to work until 5:00 pm sharp or certainly not any longer than 7 ½ minutes beyond 5. Then run, run, run home to hurry go to sleep to get up and be back at work on the second job at 11:00 pm or midnight, and would stay there until either 11:00 am the next day Saturday or 12:00 noon, Saturday. Yes, this was my life…and after getting off on Saturday, of course, I didn't go home and sleep, you know I was mom, and had stuff to do for the household, and I had a terrific guy my significant other, Pernell.

Pernell would come and visit us, when he was in New Jersey…so I'd be out and about with them doing our thing, until somewhere between 4 and 6pm, and then I'd get home to try and sleep before heading off to work. It wasn't totally bad you see because I was fortunate to have the limo pick me up on Friday and Saturday nights. How cool is that?! Way cool. Imagine hot summer nights, as sultry as they were, and this long shiny limo would pull up for me, Anita. And, of course, I was totally awesome and tired beyond compare. I would sashay out of the house, filling the air with exotic fragrances (which I secretly adore!), and dressed well, for working all night in a room by myself waiting for Europe and the Asia-Pac countries to come on line and/or waiting for something to go horribly wrong with the network. What the heck, it paid well $35.00 per hour at 24 hours per week. I could do that! You would too. Yeah cash is seductive, not for purposes of greed…but for purposes to stabilize your household to give your kid a sense of security since you're divorced. We do things as parents (especially female parents), for reasons we're not always cognizant of. Like being involved with companions that are not exactly what you really need or desire.

Mothers, I've learned sacrifice for their children, to the point of near death of themselves at times. Parenting at best, at least for me, I believe, is more than love, it is sacrificial. But, when I think of that statement, I realize that the True Love that we have been given freely, was the ultimate sacrificial love for the all of us? Yes, it was and still is and will always be. God is real in His love for us and He sent His Son for our salvation.

It was imperative for me to do a truly great job by delivering my daughter to the world so that she would be fully equipped, able and whole in her mind, body and spirit, lacking nothing. At every time that I could, I poured all that I had been given by my mom and grandmother and my childcare provider, Dorsey, into her. I wanted to rest easy in knowing that my daughter was able to care for herself and perhaps even others who would perhaps be in her charge at some point in time. That was my primary concern and goal in rearing my daughter. My mother had instilled those same principals in me as I grew under her love and diligent care.

My desire to provide for my family at times was overwhelming. I believed that if any of my family members would be the one to do so, it would be me. As a child, I was always willing and ready. I always knew I would go the distance to get the job done. I wasn't interested in being looked at as a martyr. I simply wanted and still do want the best for each and every one of them. It is my sincere desire to do for them so that they will become established and their household will be intact. So I have always prayed for the ability to do and be…more, to help another (even beyond my own bloodlines) in their situations, however that more would manifest itself whether it would be sharing of resources, time, talent, and most importantly love with an encouraging word that uplifts and inspires in times of testing and trials.

During this time, I was working as I've noted something fiercely. My salary continued to grow in leaps and bounds. I was becoming skeptical. What was really going on? One new project after another I was called upon to lead. Each one carried more weight than the next and more funds. I'd get pulled off of one and then onto a better one with an even higher compensation rate. I'm not trying to say that I was greedy. I could sense that this was beyond what I understood. I didn't know what it was. At the same time, some things began to change in me. I was tired, very tired. Obviously so, I worked all the time. My job wasn't physically strenuous. I shrugged it off initially.

I learned firsthand what it was to not have to be concerned about finances. I even FORGOT when I was to be paid. In times past, I knew every pay date for the entire year. Yes, I clearly marked it out on my day-runner. Yep sure did. I needed to know how much I could do and when I'd be able to do it or do without it. I've tried to always keep the household sound.

Sum would say 'Mommy we have extra everything.' That was a result of working as a consultant. As a consultant, you never knew when the project was going to end and as I said, I was mommy. What was I gonna do when there wasn't much money and contracts were difficult to come by? The roof, heating and cooling was always secured. However, we would also require more than a roof. Therefore, when the going was good, we would get the essentials; deodorant; toothpaste, you name it! You know how females consume! When we were in need of essentials we were always stocked up! That Mommy thing again!

Why was I driven to work so hard? No longer was there any financial instability. I'm not a greedy person. But still I was driven to work for some reason.

So here comes the ultimate position, the promotion, full-time position, excellent benefits, and a stellar opportunity! I had to interview with eight individuals in one day to get that job! Whew! There is a God in heaven. He was watching out over me, as in all times. I am here. I've arrived or so I thought…the problem was that I didn't know where I was. I didn't have a clear definition of where I was headed either. I've got twenty-five engineers reporting to me, Nellie! Yeah baby. Ummm hmmm. Sure did. This was to some folk's extreme dismay. Who is this Nellie Wosu? Why was I here at this time? My peers were resentful of me. They took me to task. My manager who had hired me was not readily available when I first came on board and it appeared for a more than a moment, that I wasn't going to be able to make it do what it do. I struggled terrifically so. It appeared that I was coming undone. I couldn't for the life of me understand what was happening.

My staff was rebellious like none I had ever worked with in previous times. On all accounts, I'm an excellent manager. One of my former managers said of me, 'Nellie is a no-

nonsense, no bull___, type of woman. She gets the job done...every time. When I'm away, I never worry about anything in this environment, she is the reason, I've been promoted several times, her sheer impact in this organization is above par.'

That man, was truly a supportive manager, he went to bat for me on several occasions. He said his father had taught him that an employee you could rely on was worth their pay. Anthony ensured that my household was well taken care of. To this day, we have remained friends. Anthony is my favorite blonde.

... *"What is man that You are mindful of him, ..."* Hebrews 2:6

Favor. Unmerited favor has been my lot. I don't brag about it, for it is nothing that I've done to deserve it. Even with all of my helping I would fail and fall miserably short. It's what I believe is truly within the confines of my heart. I genuinely have a great love for people, of all races, for humanity! I'm made of up many ethnicities; I call myself 'Heinz 57 Varieties'. And, when we think about it, perhaps we all are 57 varieties, too. The good thing is that we are all from the One and Only Source of Love, the Ultimate, God. Stating that does something to me deep down on the inside. It gives me a moment of stillness in silence letting that Truth reverberate within me. I feel it on the inside, the Love of Love. The uniting of the all of us...is through Love. How do we hate one another? How can we hate, when we've been created by and through Love? It's sorrowful and saddening to my spirit to know that hate exists in us, God's people. We're all chosen by Him, every single one of us has been chosen by Him, we belong to Him. Why do want to devalue another person's validation in Christ?

A former co-worker, Lucy, who became a very good friend, used to say "Nellie, you're a Child of the Universe"! I liked that so much…that resonated within me and still does. It's funny how people can see you better than you can sometimes see your own self.

I'm a very transparent type of person. My facial expressions reveal what is going on in my heart and mind almost at any given moment. If you want to know without question what I'm thinking about in certain situation, check my face. I cannot for some reason "mask" how I feel. I am authentic in who I am.

So, here I am with this great new position with 24/7 responsibility for two shifts. I had arrived or so I thought. Little did I know that my peer and two direct-reports one a full-timer the other a consultant were staging a coup against me. They had been filling my manager's ear with venomous lies against me.

One day, on my way in to the office, my manager apprehended me and quickly took me into a 'room' where she said she wanted to speak with me. Ok, about what I inquired. Couldn't I go put my things down first? No, no wait here. I'll be right back. She took an inordinate amount of time returning. When she did, she had the three in tow behind her. My eyes narrowed wondering what this was all about.

Well the manager that hired me, the one who had gone to get the posse to burn me at the stake, began to speak. She outlined in fine detail what she had been receiving from this three headed entity, lying telling tales about me. All lies. Absolute bold faced lies. She expounded on what each one had said to her collectively and individually about me. I grew furious. She didn't ask me to speak at all. I was speechless. When she got to a point she had requested that they each take the opportunity to address me in the concerns that they had about me and my competency in managing my staff. My manager said she believed that when someone was 'accused' that it was only fitting that the accused have an opportunity to hear out what the accusers had said regarding the accused, who in this case, was me, Nellie! And, that I would be able to defend myself against such allegations. Was this the new court of law within investment banking? This was an outrage! But God is still on the throne and in absolute charge and control.

Isaiah 54:17
No weapon formed against you shall prosper, And every tongue which rises against you in judgment You shall condemn. This is the heritage of the servants of the LORD, And their righteousness is from Me," *Says the LORD.*

Would you believe that not one of them, no not one of them, the three headed entity, could not speak. They had been rendered mute! They were not able to utter a single syllable against me? Not even a 'peep' came out…they had lost their ability to breathe and they had no voice…in fact they sat as stone statutes. Truth!

The manager became concerned. She prodded and prodded and implored them to say something, anything, just say something to me about their charges against me. She was beginning to look kind of strange herself. I was fuming. I knew what it now meant to be Daniel in the Lion's Den. The Lord, Himself, had shut their mouth. Emotion began to well up inside of me. I felt hurt and betrayed by my colleagues. Why had they done this to me? Jealously is cruel as the grave. I prayed silently for the Lord to hold back my tears and to keep me. He did it for me.

Well, the manager, by now, was totally exasperated and frustrated. I believe she felt they made her look foolish in her attempts to get them to come clean. My manager decided to bring the whole event to a close. She stated her summary discourse and forbid them from ever having those conversations with her again about me ever or with anyone for that matter. In fact, she went so far as to say to the three headed entity that they were banned from ever even bringing my name to her again, in any way shape form or fashion. She never wanted them to utter my name out of their mouth again to anyone in that corporation. And, as far as I know, they never did, with one exception, however.

She dismissed them and they got up en masse and left the conference room in silence moving as one entity with three heads.

As I sat pondering that scripture and believing what I knew to be truth, then I reckoned that the Lord would also have known where my journey would lead me, next since He is the author and finisher of my faith.

In those days, although I was a minister, I would have never thought what I knew was "discernment". It seemed that I had an uncanny ability to be in just the right place at just the right moment. Many wanted to know where I came from. My female counter parts Black and White, did not, I repeat did not like me at all for some reason they found me to be a threat to their position.

I was not timid and I spoke up for myself and anyone else who was being challenged. My mother instilled in me to always take the high road. She never let me forget that the truth would stand and a lie would fall. Mommy drove home the fact that I was to live by the Golden Rule without fail each and every single day throughout the day, every day, and beyond...until she spoke no more.

My mother's mother, Nellie, who I am named for, ensured that her children would be educated and most assuredly decent if nothing else...and that we were to always be for the underdog. Grandma said, anyone can be a winner, but what do you do, when you're not the winner this time?

Funny, it seemed that I was always a winner to me. I wasn't trying to be a winner I simply seemed to have something going for me...that I could never actually put my finger on or define. Something that caused me to speak my mind in truth...always causing someone else to reconsider a negative action or attitude. My childhood friend, Dawn, always said I was her conscious. I recall I've always had a very strong burning like desire to do what is right and to help others do same, also. I like to help.

Now don't get me wrong, I was certainly no saint...not by a long shot...a very long shot at that. That's the truth. I was dead wrong on many occasions. In fact, in days of old, they would have gathered me up and stoned me and my shadow. But, somehow I always wound up saving the day and being saved, too.

Jeremiah 1:5

"Before I formed you in the womb I knew you; Before you were born I sanctified you; I ordained you a prophet to the nations."

4 THE DIAGNOSIS

Needless to say, I'm holding tight and fast, and have been for several hours since I went to the doctor on Saturday morning at 8:30 am. Now, it's Sunday, afternoon, I'm getting worse. I can't speak and I'm turning colors, I'm turning gray. The nurses are working on me like wild fire. I'm holding on as long as I can and as tight as I can. I hear that voice. *Let go. I think I can't let go. I've got to hold on. The Voice. Let go. I can't let go was the thought in my head. I've got to hold on. I can hold on. The Voice said, I have this. Let go now. I can't let go. No. I won't let go. You will let go the Voice said in my head. No!* By that time, I'm struggling hard, they're bringing in machines fast and furious, people are all in the room, all around, asking me questions, I can't speak, I can't breathe. Some asks about oxygen for me. At that time, I look up and see Summer and her classmate Yashika coming into the room. I think Lord have mercy. Please don't let her see this. Please don't let them experience this. This what? *Anita, let it go! You can't hold it any longer, release it. Trust me, I am with you.* I'm now crying tears running down my face. I'm pleading God have mercy. He said, *I do. Let go Anita, let it go.* So I did and I couldn't stop it. Fluid came out of every orifice in my body, the fluid erupted with such violent force from my mouth the nurses were drenched in my bodily fluids. I had let go. I had come

THE KEEPER OF ME

undone…completely. The rest was fade to black. I'm not sure when I came around. That was my first foray into my new home, the hospital. I was there for almost four weeks. It was there that I later learned that my lungs had collapsed, and that I had pneumonia, and I also had something called, CHF, Congestive Heart Failure, Stage IV. I also learned that I had an Ejection Fraction (EF) of 35% which was the hearts ability to pump. Later I would learn that there is no cure for CHF. And, that the life expectancy with the disease was 5 years. I was 39 years old. Lord please have mercy on me.

After that, and a few more extended stays in the hospital, several months later, I got fired! That final straw came as a result in February 2000, when my dearly beloved Uncle Fred, had transitioned and I was going to attend his funeral in Concord, to be by my Aunt Cue's side. My manager would have no parts of it. He warned me that there would be consequences if I did go for "just an uncle's funeral". I went to my Uncle's funeral. There were consequences, I'm glad there were, I was able to live with myself. My Uncle Fred had been the acting father in my life since my own Daddy had died when I was five years old. Now here I was on the verge of being 40, and this manager man was going to threaten me, Anita, about going to Uncle Fred's funeral to be with my family. Not today Jack!

According to my manager, 'Your staff needs you Nellie.' You're not here enough you've been out too much, more than you are here.' I tried to defend myself, he wouldn't have anything to do with the subject. We had remote capabilities, which I utilized when I wasn't there. Even after the funeral, there I was sick as a dog, with that laptop plugged up to the phone line (oh yeah, I remember dial-up!) working with my staff giving them orders to work the help desk effectively.

Also at that same time, I was in the process of purchasing a home, and had to let that go. It wouldn't be prudent to purchase a home without a job, even if you did have a fat bank account.

So after the funeral I returned to work within a reasonable time. Once again, I began to have those thoughts again, what are you going to do with your life? Is this all there is I wondered silently to myself? My friend Chris, had said to me, 'Nellie you don't have a job, you have a position.' I did? What position, favorite corporate slave? Do you have a life worth living?

Soon, I learned that I did have a life worth living by becoming a member of the unemployed. Boy was I relieved! I had just about had enough. They gave me a pre-paid severance of about 8 grand…and said adios!

So, by now, you must know that there's a name that one would call me. Yep, I'm a holic. Workaholic, you know it by now, I'm not good without something to do, daily. I'm good for about five months and I go stir crazy. I've got to get another job! And, I did, get the job and went into salary overdrive! What????? Are you kidding me???

Even seasoned professionals were not making this type of money! I knew I did a fabulous job. I was capable with joy and laughter, serious as cancer about my work. I was competent beyond measure. I excelled against the stacked odds, even while out of breath. Every review, I far exceeded requirements or exceeded requirements, every time! I'm not bragging I was serious about my work. If I was there and I was there, I was there for the whole entire Black female population.

All of my professional career, I had worked in white male dominated fields. I knew if they let me in and I did an excellent job, that others could come behind me. If I failed, others would not be able to join in the adventure to corporate success. I wasn't there just for me I was there for my gender and my sisters who were of color, from various parts of the globe, especially the exceptional ones who were in full effect, if you catch my drift. They were my female counterparts. I believed in my role as the Encouraging One who would and did dispel the myths!

That manager, that I told you about who had made inquisition of the three headed entity, knew me, I believe from before my entry into technology. She knew of me when I was a research assistant in investment banking where I worked for five major investment bankers that headed up the Dutch-German, Scandinavian, Japan,

Australia, London and Paris efforts. By the time of our next meeting more than ten years would have passed.

I looked somewhat different, however, my name was still the same, and remains such to this day, Nellie A. Wosu. I am the only one in these United States with that name. The manager knew of my abilities and she did let people know that Nellie is one of the leading female forces in Technology, she marveled at my tenacity in achieving such success, for a black woman, without what she deemed, help. What she didn't know was that I had always had Help.

I was able to do what I did without ever making a wave ripple in the pond, with the exception of always being in the right place at the right time with the desire to bring someone else along to fulfill their destiny too. My job is to help you get there and stay with you for a period of time, and then to always speak a word to cause someone to rethink. That's favor from God. He has given me good success in all of the endeavors and assignments He's sent me to work on.

5 HOSPITAL VISITS AM I

After the three headed entity debacle I was about done with the corporate way of doing things. Something was changing inside of me. Why was I thinking these thoughts? Who was putting these thoughts in my head? I liked my work. Yeah, I know I was tired, but I liked my work. I liked other things that I did, too. I loved teaching in Church. Yes, even as busy as I was, I always made time to go to Church. And, when I worked on those Saturday nights until Sunday mid-morning, I would take the limo to Church and later catch the bus home or I would have lunch or early dinner with a friend and then get a ride home

My frequent trips to the hospital for extended ad nauseam stays had become burdensome. Nearly every 1 ½ - 2 weeks, I would wind up in the hospital for 3-4 weeks at a time. The doctors couldn't find any reason as to why this was happening to me. Everything was out of kilter. I was getting weaker and weaker. Not wanting to let onto my employer that I was "sick". I played the game quietly. I couldn't breathe. So I developed a new persona, I became somewhat aloof and kept quiet. Still doing a good job I was. But remember I'd been singed. So it was expected that I would become detached. I wasn't detached. I couldn't breathe and I didn't want anyone to know about it! I covered up my growing and pressing health matters. The doctor's office became my second home. My work day was a staggering 12-14 hours a day. After hitting the wall earlier that year, I no longer worked two jobs. I couldn't hold it any longer. I had just one job for the first time in a very long time. I couldn't get enough rest and my favorite motto had become "oooh child, I'm worn out". I didn't know why I was worn out.

Never letting anyone know I had CHF, I was acting suspect, I attempted to avoid everyone by hankering down with my work. Rarely did I raise my head to talk to anyone. I didn't want them to notice that when I would speak I would get winded easily. And, then something else began to occur, I would get in mid-sentence, and forget what I needed to say. Me, lightning tongue Anita?! Quick with an answer was I always until now. I felt I was losing something within me and I wasn't quite sure how to handle this matter.

Later, I would learn that new symptom was a result of lack of oxygen when I slept. Now, I had something else to contend with, Obstructed Sleep Apnea. After I had the sleep study, it confirmed that I had Obstructed Sleep Apnea. The doctor said I had "a lot of apneas", the diagnosis helped to explain why I was so tired all of the time, which wasn't helping the CHF.

By now, I'm a regular at just about every hospital in the local community in two states. Congestive Heart Failure is a devil. It comes upon you without warning. One minute you're fine! The next minute your body is swelling and you can't breathe. The ambulance is coming they're placing oxygen in your nostrils. You go to the hospital they dry you out with IV-Lasix, they hook you up and put a Foley catheter on you and you're good. Good, that is until you go home and after that you're back at the hospital again in about 1 ½ weeks! Stop. Repeat Steps 1-3 and follow through again. This time try flat lining for kicks!

Yes, flat lining. Clinically dead. No brain waves or heartbeat. Flat lining has occurred to me so many times that I now simply say that I have flat lined more than three times. When I used to say the actual amount of times it had occurred to me. People became weirded out and would run from me, literally and figuratively, too.

We were saved because of my infirmity!

Evangelist Moody used to say to me, 'Nellie, God has a hedge of protection around you.' I would agree wholeheartedly. I was never sure why, though, until my journey with heart disease became my purpose and calling and my new raison d'être, for His glory and to the benefit of many, including me.

Summer was in her last year of high school, and she needed directions as to how she would get to school on the train. She wasn't too familiar with taking the train so I told her we would ride together in the morning, as I had a meeting scheduled in New York, in the World Trade Center, way up on the upper floors.

Divine Intervention?!

I believe I mentioned how CHF can put you down when it wants to without warning. Such came in the middle of a particular night. I had a frightful night of battling with my health and matters of my heart. It was unreal. I was tormented beyond measure. The Air-Sep machine and C-PAP, were not working for me this time. I was spent. Worn out and dead was I. I walked the floor all night long trying to get air. None could be found. Finally, I went to the living room, and there I battled with the devil to let me be, in the name of Jesus. There are times, when you simply have to take a stand about what's happening to you. You can't just let the devil run rip shod against you. We have been given the power to tread on serpents. So, I called a moratorium on the enemy devil who was messing with me. I had to rest, I needed rest. I was so very tired and exhausted. I had to get up in the morning and take care of things. I yelled I must get some rest and sleep, in Jesus' name. So, I lay down and slept. The thing was that when I woke up, I couldn't move. I was paralyzed from my neck down. I kid you not. I couldn't move. I struggled and it was as if I was encased in cement. I became alarmed. At about that time, I heard Sum. Summer jumped up from having overslept. Mom she yelled, get up. We've got to go. I'm going to be late for school. I told her no she wouldn't just hurry up and get ready. She wanted to know what about me, get up mom you're going to go with me, remember? Yes, I do. I don't feel too well Summer, you

45

go on and I'll show you perhaps tomorrow. She looked at me funny. Ma what's wrong? Nothing. (Sound familiar). I'm just tired. Mom, why are you lying there like that? Just tired Sum. I'm good. It's about 6:00 am or so. So she readies herself reluctantly, and starts out the door. Mom, come lock the door. Oh Sum, go ahead and lock it. Mom! I'm gonna miss my bus! No, you're not...lock the security door good and I'll see you when you get home. Make sure you lock both doors. I'm in the living room lying on the sofa encased in cement from the neck down just looking at her, not moving a muscle. Mom are you okay, you look funny? Who wouldn't look funny after the night I've had, I said to her. Ah, Ma, I'm sorry. Go, go have a good day Button, love you big! Love you too, she says, and closes the door and I hear her lock both doors. Great kid, I think to myself, I'll miss her.

Today, is September 11, 2001, and I'm paralyzed from my neck down. My child doesn't know about this I think. She's on her way to school, and here I am when she comes back I may be just dead completely. Lord have mercy, Christ have mercy, Lord have mercy on me. I fall into some kind of deep sleep.

I am jolted awake by the loud ringing of the phone and sunlight is flooding into the room. Where, where, where is it, the phone, where is it? Oh, crap, it's over there on the other side of room, I bolt up to get it just before it stops ringing. Anita, Anita, Anita, are you okay? Tracy, my cousin was screaming through the phone. I was worried sick about you, she said. What? I'm fuzzy in my thinking, then I recall, how did I get over here? I remembered what had happened in the morning, I couldn't move. I was paralyzed. Now, I'm moving. I check myself. Tracy goes onto explain, didn't you hear? I thought you were on your way to work. I was worried sick. Why? I wondered. Do you have the TV on? No. Turn it on, turn it on! Okay. I go over and turn it on. And, I see it. My eyes open wide. I think oh God, no. Summer! Tracy, I've got to go. I've got to see about Summer! She left this morning to go to school. Anita, you can't drive. I know, I know. I'll call Adriane. And, I did call Adriane. I tell Adriane, she's seen everything, too, on the TV. Adriane, I'm coming to your house now, I'll drive my car to you, you drive us to Summer's school. Adriane lived two blocks from me. Summer went to school in Hoboken, NJ, which is just across the Hudson River from downtown, New York. Adriane and I are moving at the speed of light on Ocean Avenue in Jersey City, we get at the bridge that shows a direct view over to the World Trade Center, we scream collectively at the sight. The second tower is gone! Oh God, what is happening? Adriane is stunned. Adriane, Adriane, let's go! Adriane steps on it. We get there, in Hoboken, the police are everywhere. We can't get into Hoboken the usual way. They are blocking the way into the area to drive up in Hoboken. So, we go the "other way" to get in. No cops here yet to keep us out. We drove several blocks, I rush into the school. Students, the Sisters and parents are gathered all around. Where's Summer? Mrs. Wosu, she's downstairs somewhere, the Sister said?

I race-run in my best efforts to get to her, Summer, I'm calling out, Summer. Mom? What's wrong. Long sigh. Mom? All of the students had not been told yet. Summer was talking with her classmate. They were talking about having to say extra prayers for some reason this morning in Chapel.

Mommy what's wrong why are you here? I look at her dead straight in her eyes, and say "we're under siege, we've been attacked, the World Trade Center has been hit. The Towers are down." What?! Summer and her classmate, are floored. They begin to vibrate. Hold yourself. Hold yourself. I say, everything will be fine. Silently praying, God please let this be truth. Hold yourself I thought to my own self, as I came into full awareness, I was supposed to be there in meetings, today! Lord, what is it? Why has this happened? Thoughts are racing in my head? No answers.

By that time the classmate begins to tear up and comes undone, naturally. She said her father worked in the World Trade Center. I'm concerned for her I console her to the best of my ability. My gifting came into effect immediately, that feeling, that feeling when my body starts to do its own thing and I get warm and tingling sensation runs all over me, like electrical stimuli it feels warm, but I feel cool and warm inside all at the same time. I can't make it happen, it

48

just happens for some reason by itself and I start to change somehow. Standing still, I look at her, up and down, all around, she's looking at me, I start that staring deeper, like I seeing beyond, it's happening to me this time very strongly, I began to probe and feel her in the Spirit. I don't sense her father's presence around her at all. If he had been stricken in some way, I believe, his spirit would have been all over her. It was not there. There was simply light around her, as in protecting her. I told her emphatically that everything was quite fine with her father. I reassured her of that. Not certain as to how I knew that to be so. But, I knew I could "feel" that Truth as I went into her Spirit and saw that light surrounding her. Later we learned that yes, her father was unharmed and was totally well. God had done it again, and, let me be a part of Him. OK, but, why me? Then I heard inside my head and heart my mother's voice, with a duplicate voice, the same voice that puts the questions in my head all the time, that voice was in sync with mommy's voice, and I heard "why not you?" in seeming oneness. I became still and pondered, why not me, what.

Not understanding fully, I was happy and we rejoiced, but then my mind trailed and began to ponder inside. How could I have known these things? They were not wishful thinking. Something was happening to me. I was changing somehow. I could sense it just as I was sensing my rapidly growing weakness in my physical body. My intuition and Spirit became stronger as my physical self, began to wane.

49

That thing that sensation that power would take me over, maybe, this is the way the heart works, when it starts to go south, I thought.

2 Corinthians 12:9
And He said to me, "My grace is sufficient for you, for My strength is made perfect in weakness." Therefore most gladly I will rather boast in my infirmities, that the power of Christ may rest upon me.

As per usual, I become sick again, and have to delay returning to work. Previously, there had been a merger with another company and there was an overlap in staffing and thus we had too much duplication in personnel. Now, as you would expect after the heinous events of 9-11, the pressure was coming down hard and they (my company) began pressing me to return to work. Eventually, I was able to obtain permission from my physicians that it would be suitable for me to return to work. Immediately, I reported this information to my manger and he stopped his incessant phone calls and emails to me. I thought it a bit odd that he no longer had any further communication with me at all. I emailed him on several occasions and he never responded. Odd quite odd, indeed. I attempted to phone others at work, no response. So as anyone would do, on the scheduled return to work day, I return ready to begin yet again. Not happening! Nope, not today Nellie. Puzzled look on my face, as all of the employees are whizzing by going through the turnstile. I'm stopped abruptly. Why? Well, my Cardkey wouldn't respond in the proper manner. That is to say it no longer had the credentialing to indicate it was safe for me to go through the turnstile. Security was puzzled, so was I. They examined the card to see if it was bent…nope wasn't bent. Checked the expiration. All clear. What's going on? Let's get the supervisor of the database and look at your profile. Ah, yes. You need to report to HR. Hmmm, I thought okay…perhaps they want the original medical permission to return to work form. Yep that's it, I thought. WRONG!!!!!!!!

Absolutely wrong, was I. I was quickly carted off to HR in an area that I wasn't even familiar with. Ushered into a conference room, told to wait here. Oh and yes, would you like something to drink? No thank you. My mind was racing. What could this be about? Well just wait you'll soon find out, said the Voice in my head. It will be alright, don't worry, said the Voice. Long sigh. Okay if you say so. So this lovely young woman comes in to greet me and has with her a stack of papers in a file about ½ mile high they're all for me. Whoopdee Doo!!! Whoopdee Doo!!! We no longer have use for you!!! Yes, we no longer have use for you, Nellie Wosu.

6 HIS PROMISE & PROVISION

The Lord promises to be with us always. In His word we learn the truth that He will not leave us nor forsake us ever. He's promised to be with us even unto the end. How many times have we thought we were counted out, doomed, done with, finished, kaput only to see that God has always had something greater in store for us.

We may have gone over the edge but His saving grace kept us from falling. When we believed we could go no further He did more for us in ways that were not even comprehensible for our very limited thinking mind and heart.

Such has been the case for me since my diagnosis with heart disease. And, I am certain that I'm the better for it, even though it didn't always seem to be that nor actually did I want it to be that, at times. Yes, misery does love company. The good thing is that I for some reason had a desire to not want it to be over just yet. I knew what the diagnosis and prognosis was. It was very bleak and had not one ounce of cure. Not embracing that truth of the physician's report, but acknowledging it to a degree, somehow, I kept on even with little and fledgling faith. As a result of that little faith I've made it by faith and the faith is strong and big. My faith had become bigger than my fears.

Knowing Him and accepting His way as the way for me, I am better in ways that go beyond what I or survey could have hoped for on any given day. There were times of deep physical distress and turmoil, lack of funds, lack of loved ones and you name it. It was hard for me to physically hold the Bible in my hands. I would listen to the scripture in my head, certain scriptures would automatically rise up in me and I'd be "kept" again and would receive a modicum of relief in that moment. I'm convinced that it is essential that we when we are able to assemble ourselves with other believers in our places of worship, we grow strong in our hearts and minds, individually and collectively. The Lord is to be experienced in all of His magnificent splendor. If you're able to, press your way to get to His house. Both the one in this physical realm and the one right there in the protected space of your body, that being your heart and encourage your mind to follow. Let your heart lead your mind, not your mind lead your heart for one is spiritual and the other at times is not even logical.

Romans 10:17
So then faith comes by hearing, and hearing by the word of God.

I'll ask you to consider your present situation and ask yourself what it is that you desire from Him. Not desires of material possession, but desires for hope, wellness, the giving away of self and for serving unselfishly? What would you do for Him to benefit others and glorify God?

Our best attempt at coping often time is wrought with fluctuating belief and faith. When we are used to doing things in our own power, we believe that we are capable of slaying the giant. However, we may be able to slay the giant, but that too, is not without God's work in our situation. Acknowledging that power of the Lord is not something we do enough of. Even for the believer of Him, there are times when we think to ourselves and may even demonstrate in our actions, "I've got this". Oh yeah, you do? Good let me see you work this out now.

Not realizing that there are situations in life that come at us fast, hard and before quick can get the message we're blindsided. All of sudden without any rhyme or reason, we've been taken out of the game that we've been playing and playing good.

As you've heard me say in the previous pages that occurred to me on that Saturday when I couldn't get up from the bed and there appeared to be a slab of lead placed upon my chest. From that time to any time since and I suppose and believe for the rest of my existence in this time, I'm forever changed in ways that are beyond my greatest understanding. I've accepted many of the changes that have occurred in my life. That wasn't always the way it was. It's not so much that I wrestled with these changes I just had a difficult time from time to time wondering why this was happening to me. What did I do to get this situation? Well the fact of the matter is what did I do to

NOT get this situation? The actual and true response is that this is what I'm to get at this juncture in my life and it's not for me or about me. But rather how I deal with the situation at hand, leaning not on my own understanding but trusting that and this too shall pass. A brighter day will come even though the storm clouds are closing in and I'm beaten and burdened, I hurt, and I may even be angry with God…that at this time, I am being challenged like this for no good reason.

Oh yes, that was the internal rage. He knew it and I felt it. My lament was not left unheard and felt by Him. He brought to me conversations in my head from when I was growing up, they were conversations with my mother, where she had told me of many trials and tribulations in her life, and how she was able to hold on and believe by faith in God. She told me to always be ready to serve in whatever capacity I was being led. Even in the capacity when I would have to be the one to bear the weight of trials. Every day is not sunny a day in our life. The truth is that every day the sun is shining in some part of the world and we can take consolation knowing that the sun will rise in just a few hours again in our neck of the woods.

Mommy would say that the Lord is too wise to make a mistake and too just to be unkind. She was absolutely right. I've accepted that truth little by little to the point of my embracing it wholeheartedly. His ways are not our ways.

If we would take a different perspective in dealing with hard situations and truths in our life then we could see from this vantage point; "in our mind's eye", which is the eye where we obtain vision from Spirit.

God's provision for us is such that we will never lack anything.

Psalm 84:11
For the LORD God is a sun and shield; The LORD will give grace and glory; No good thing will He withhold From those who walk uprightly.

In all times, I've attempted to walk uprightly. Of course, I've failed miserably at times, deliberately so. Those were times when I chose to not walk uprightly. Perhaps in those moments I didn't want to be held accountable for certain things that had occurred. I decided to take the zero. I found that when you're constantly walking upright that you invoke the ire of others who are jealous of you because of your desire to do what is right in your daily walk. No the things I did were not heinous but I took on a so-what type of attitude. One co-worker years ago before all of these matters came into my life, told me emphatically, "Nellie why do you have to care so much? You want to be everyone's mother." The truth is that I do care much for people, for the human race. I care sincerely about what matters in your life. I listened to the irrational voice saying no one cares about you that way, why should you care that way about them?

Enough already. I realized in time that I am my brother and sister's keeper. That we are to love one another. We may not always like what we do or the way people treat us this is true. However, the real truth is that we've been commanded to love one another as our self. Know that obedience is truly better than sacrifice.

Having come to full acceptance and understanding of His grace, mercy, love and provision has placed me in a position to let go and let God. Knowing God for yourself through the sacrifices made by His Son our Lord, Jesus Christ, places us if we'll desire to be in that place to assist another who may also be going through a challenging time.

I must say that the more I gave back, the paying it forward in word and deed, helped me to reprioritize my situation. And, without even knowing it I was being healed of the burden of my lament that sought to have me inextricably bound to defeat in my circumstances. If you want to know how truly blessed you are, go visit the hospital and just stroll and take a look to your left and to your right as you meander through the unit. Yes, you will rejoice in your situation while rejoicing that this is only a test and you've been setup to pass the test of your life!

Today is your day to rededicate the remainder of your life to living within your full ability and purpose on purpose! It doesn't matter whether you have Stage I – II – III or IV of whatever type of catastrophic illness you have. Just know that the life you have is for His glory and to the benefit of others even unto yourself, and watch His provision run and take you over!

You may not be able to do things the way in which you had done them previously. However, you're enabled to be something else and do more than you would expect. I've actually come to believe that is just simply a very good thing. I also believe when you come to this understanding and acceptance you, too, will be exceedingly pleased with yourself in your ability to be enabled with the desire to still do and be simultaneously in your new life and no longer look at your past as being the best time in your life. The best time in your life is right now for you can make this time whatever you want it to be for you and those around you to! Catch the notion that you are better than your former self. Look at where He's already brought you from…my oh my! Can't you see where's He's leading you to. I learned this by going back to the video tape in my head and I saw something greater on the landscape for me…it wasn't always clear…but I could certainly see the Light in my situation.

I am reminded of this scripture which is loaded with an expectancy that causes a big sigh of relief and joy in my heart knowing that I will not fail in this trial and tribulation of Congestive Heart Failure. The victory is already mine and it is yours too in your situation! Let us embrace this truth together as brothers and sisters knowing what when we believe in His promise and provision we've already received the prize before its manifestation.

Philippians 3:12-14

Pressing Toward the Goal

*Not that I have already attained, or am already perfected; but I press on, that I may lay hold of that for which Christ Jesus has also laid hold of me. Brethren, I do not count myself to have apprehended; but one thing **I do**, forgetting those things which are behind and reaching forward to those things which are ahead, I press toward the goal for the prize of the upward call of God in Christ Jesus.*

7 THE PROCEDURE

Having now been out of work for a time and needing to get a grasp on my health agenda. I thought I'd be able to take myself on a little trip for my birthday and do some much needed soul searching. Today was my 42nd birthday! Yay, happy birthday to me!

Summer was settled in at school, Pernell had visited and returned to work. So, here I was home alone wondering (that Voice was there again) what I was going to do with my life. Well I'm going on vacation I announced out loud to no one in particular, because I was the only one there in the house or so I thought. Really? Where are you going? I heard the Voice say in my head. Not sure I said out loud. But I'm going to Newark first and then I'll decide where I'm going. The reason I was going to Newark first is because Newark, NJ is the hub for all forms of transportation; buses, trains and planes. I just needed to get there first and where ever I decided I'd take myself to that destination via one of those forms of transportation. You'll notice I still had a reasonable amount of liquidity to enable me to take on such an odd and uncustomary way of doing things. I'm generally always process driven, step one leads to step two leads to, well you get what I mean. So this was unheard of for me. Well I'd decided that's what I would do. Now to pack some stuff for about a week or so and I'd be ready to go. Packed quite well I did, not too much but nice stuff for what seemed to be warm weather...was I going to go to Florida or Cali? Hmmm, could be in Cali in about six hours or Florida in two! Hmmm, yeah that's it! California Sunshine! Okay now, let's get showered and ready to go on my birthday soiree all by my wittle self! Life is good!!!

With my traveling clothes all laid out I go turn on the shower. Whoa what was that? Whew. I turned around and almost lost my balance. Slow down I heard the Voice say in my head. Look, I'm going on vacation I've got to go. Slow down. Deep breath is very shallow. Long sigh. Girl get in the shower and get out, get dressed and get out of here, I thought to myself. Okay. Water on, adjust to my setting needed it cooler than normal for some reason. Started lathering up with my bath fragrance. I'm feeling good aren't I? Ugh, yeah? No, you're not feeling good Anita, the Voice said matter in a of fact type of way. I started not being able to catch my breath and started leaning on the wall of the shower again. I reminded myself that I must look very silly rolling up against the shower wall. How many times will this happen again and again this has happened too many hundreds of times…always resulting in the same thing. Can't breathe, somebody please take me to the hospital. No Lord not now not again. Please just let me be able to breathe and go and have a nice time and live my life. I'M TIRED AND SO VERY TIRED OF THIS NOT FEELING WELL ALL THE TIME DAY IN AND DAY OUT, WHEN WILL IT BE OVER…I'M SICK OF THIS!!! I'm angry now because I can't breathe and I'm moving at a snail's pace, too. I finish taking my shower the best I can, get out, get dressed and called my older woman friend and neighbor, Chris Cooper, and ask her to take me to the hospital. She sighs and asks me, "which one Nellie?" I pause and reluctantly say, Newark Beth Israel. It's the only hospital I hadn't been to yet. And, of course, I'd go in for a few they'd hook me up give me some more meds and I'd be on my way on my vacation, after all Newark Beth Israel is in Newark! Yay, I felt better. So Chris tells me she'll be ready in a few and asks if I'm ready I say yes letting her know I was already ready. Chris is a great friend we were co-workers when I was 15 years old and our friendship grew through the years. I'm her adopted daughter she always says. Her family is like second family to me!

Chris arrives and we're off to the ER at Newark Beth. We're there in about 20 minutes or less from Jersey City. Chris drops me off and is gone on her way. I stand outside looking at the ER entrance wanting to run, heck I can barely walk now. Run where I think sarcastically, you're not even able to breathe let alone run. It won't always be like this the Voice said in my head. Somehow I believe that not sure why though.

Go on go in and get yourself checked in. Long sigh again. According to my cousin Tracy, 'buckup Bucko'. Bucko is bucked up and drags her suitcase behind her. Dressed up, I am as usual. I go into the ER all heads turn and look at me. Perfume flying off of me like aftershocks. I walk up to the ER attendant and say I'd like to be seen. Why I'm asked. I can't breathe is my response. The attendant looks at me rather suspiciously. I look okay. Dressed to the nines even pulling tapestry luggage. Looks like I should be checking in at The Palms or someplace like that. Those were my plans actually [cynical thought]. The attendant asks the standard questions. Then I say I have Congestive Heart Failure, Stage IV. I get the look. The long stare of stop lying. Lady I can't breathe. Go and have a seat and someone will be with you shortly. The other folks waiting stare at me with hard suspicious eyes. I know they're wondering what's wrong with her. I'm uncomfortable being there. I want to go now. Maybe I'll just leave. I start to stand get myself together I'm getting out of here. Don't want to be here anyway. I don't like this place. Going back home NOW. I'll be okay just like always. As I'm about to pull my luggage I'm beckoned to come right this way, the Triage Nurse motioning for me to come quickly. The others in the ER waiting room look at me like who in the world are you. I don't know who I am, I think to myself, where is Anita, where did SHE go? When will she be back?! I'm not the same anymore. I don't know who I am anymore.

The Triage Nurse hits me with a battery of questions I respond robotically I know the drill. She's amazed that I know every medication, every date I've been hospitalized and the duration of same for the past several years, every test I've taken and the results. I'm fully versed in the medical terminology. She hooks me up for an EKG looks at me strange well you get the drift. Yeah, yeah, yeah admit me again. Now, I've got a new hospital under my belt. Hmmm, whatdaya think about that little girl?

Nothing I think other than this is the hospital where my mother died after her heart surgery. Now I'm here. No one knows I'm here except Chris and she drives off into the sunshine. Long pause and sigh. Don't worry everything will work out okay I hear the voice say in a reassuring manner.

Three weeks later I'm checking out of the hospital. Guess I did go on vacation. Return home feeling better after having been drained with IV Lasix for a period of time, standard regimen for heart failure at least in those days, this was September 2002.

The staff at Newark Beth was great! I enjoyed myself. I had very few visitors if any at that time. People have families, jobs and other pressing matters in their daily lives. My family lived not in the general area. My daughter was away in her first year of college. I'm divorced and my significant other is an over-the-road driver. So I'm here with me, myself and I and host of cardiology staff which I learn by name since I'm here for the entire rotation of staff. Bye Nellie take good care of yourself! Bye, I will, I promise I will. I tried, I actually tried to take care of myself the best I could.

Before two weeks came I was on the non-breathing thing again. Foiled again! C-Pap not working, Air-Sep not helping…all meds are at maximum dosage…160 mg. of Lasix daily. Toprol XL, Aldactone, you name it I'm on it!

So what other recourse do I have except to go back there again to Newark Beth. Okay what the heck, I'll go there again. I heeded the Voice in my head. I no longer had the strength to fight back any further. I was weakening further rapidly so for some reason.

I pack my bag again this time not for a vacation but for my monthly drying out session. It's like I'm in a type of rehab program after falling off the wagon. I fell off because I couldn't breathe and I'm weak. My motto is "ooooh child I'm worn out". That's me worn out.

So, they recognize me they think when the staff makes their rounds. Good morning. Good morning I respond. It looks like you had a pretty rough go of it last night. Yes. That would be about right. Weren't you just here recently? Yes, about 1 ½ weeks ago. Long stare. Standard information given again. So tired of this. Can't you just look at the records and know what to put? No they can't. Each visit is separate and must be treated as if it's the first time. And, if something else needs to be done, then it will be done at that time and NOT before. Later that day I'm told that doctor somebody has been reviewing my chart and history and will be in to see me later today. Okay, fine with me I say and then I shrug my shoulders…nothing new in this land.

Here Comes the Before

Enter Dr. Arroyo. This new doctor talks with me extensively about my health condition pertaining to my heart and my diabetes, which was diagnosed in 1996. He delves deep into what has happened in the physical aspects of my heart pertaining to heart failure. The doctor spent an unusual amount of time learning all about me and asking what seemed like 1000s of questions that no other doctor had ever asked me. I responded candidly to everything he asked…and he asked EVERYTHING. He wanted to know about my life, what was important to me. How I had felt prior to my diagnosis and what had been the treatment process and the like. I have always nearly had 100% recall it didn't fail me at this time. Thank God for the mind that is enabled to both recall and forget and forgive without malice.

Dr. Arroyo then proceeded to tell me about a "clinical trial" that is being performed at Newark Beth in the Cardiology Heart Failure area of the hospital and all that it entailed. He explained in great detail the intensity of the trial and what may or may not happen.

He gave me time to think about all he had explained to me and said he would return at another time to further talk with me and to answer any questions or concerns I had.

Now this was just an FYI meeting. This was not a do you want to be a part of this trial. No one could recommend me specifically no matter what happened. The trial was randomized. Therefore, I would have to pass a series of intensive and invasive tests to determine if I would even be eligible to be considered to be placed in to the "coin toss" so to speak to see whether I would be selected for several options that were available in the trial. Ground work had not yet been laid. We were in the this is what needs to be done. The thing was I would be the only determinate at this time to whether I would be able to continue on. There were stringent restrictive requirements in order to be considered. One such requirement was that there could be no blockages of the arteries and veins to the heart. To determine such a Cardiac Catheterization had to be performed. A timed walking test had to also be performed. It's important to note that I had little to no breath at this time. I had could barely walk three feet without stopping to catch my breath. This timed test would have not any breaks in walking out the allotted minutes at a rather brisk pace. There could be no stop then restart. There were also other tests that had to be taken which I'm not at liberty to discuss.

I prayed a lot before these tests and asked God to give me strength in Jesus' name to be able to successfully complete the tests so that at least I would be able to be possibly considered. I heard in my head my mother's voice saying, I'm trying to do something to help myself get better. Funny that is what Mommy said when she made the decision to have her triple by-pass surgery. She had Angina.

One of the major objectives by the developers of the device for the clinical trial was for the patients to have a better quality of life. When I heard that my ears began to perk up because I had lost my zest for living. You've heard that Fanny Lou Hammer said she was sick and tired of being sick and tired. I had gone beyond that scenario. By the time all of this had happened I'd been down to death's door more than a few times and had even entered and walked through for a period of time with all of the flat lining that I had experienced more than three times. For some reason I was always sent back.

This clinical trial was under the auspices of the FDA, Food and Drug Administration and was seeking approval for the device called the Acorn CorCap Support Device. It was a proprietary mesh netting that was designed to be used in various types of heart failure patients to passively reduce the size of the heart over a period of time. The device was being used in parts of Europe.

When my CHF was initially diagnosed my ejection fraction was 35%. Now, at this time I received new information concerning my heart's pumping ability it had plummeted to the 10% range. Anyone who knows the least amount about CHF Stage IV with an EF of 10%, knows that it's about time for lights out Nellie. That's a wrap babe. It's been real. I was solemn when I learned of this numerical nightmare.

I thought to myself is that all there is of me? Just 10% left. What can I do with 10% of me?

Matthew 19:26
But Jesus looked at them and said to them, "With men this is impossible, but with God all things are possible."

It's not what I can do with 10%, it's what God can do with 10%. He requires a tenth from us. As the widow gave her last, I too, gave all that I had left of me, which in this physical realm was what was left of my heart 10%, so that I gave to Him because I wanted to see His possible. Therefore I took a leap of faith and decided to continue on with the remaining tests.

My Clinical Trial Coordinator for the procedure and device was Jesus (Jessie) Casida. Jessie was phenomenal in every way. He was caring and concerned about how I was managing under the new type of stress I was going through. In fact, the entire staff of Cardiology professionals, at Newark Beth, are in a class by themselves. I'm not simply saying that. It was in everything they did and said to me. I could not only see it I could "feel" that what mattered to me mattered to them too. This is not always the case in patient/doctor relationships.

If you're in a relationship with your medical professional team and you're concerns are not being met or considered then, I strongly suggest, that you fire them post haste. And, commence to finding another team that will address your concerns and treat you as an individual and not group you into a pool of patient stats. You're unique and I bet your concerns of medical importance are too.

Remember YOU ARE the Leader of your medical agenda. The medical teams are to assist you in your quest to achieve wellness and your job is to be compliant, diligent while staying balanced in a positive light. When you have concerns voice them no matter how invalid you may think they are. If they don't listen…well you know what a pink slip is.

It's October 2002, I'm at Newark Beth for my second time. Now undergoing tests for possible inclusion to be considered a candidate for the clinical trial. I've been here for several weeks by now. My room has changed a few times. I'm in seventh heaven I have a private room like a little studio. My nurse tells me she knows I'm feeling better. And, I say how do you know that? She said you have your lipstick on and smiled at me! I DID have my lipstick on! I hadn't had it on in a very long time. Anyone who knows me, knows I love my lipstick, the brights: bright oranges, luscious pinks and the classic red hot oh la la reds!

See what I mean? They get to know you there at Newark Beth and know what matters to you as an individual! What other hospital nurse would pay such attention?! To something that was important to how I felt about myself as a person, a woman who wanted desperately to still be alive and soar with radiant health their staff was cognizant of those concerns.

Every day I would start my day a little delayed. I preferred to eat my breakfast first after the usual battery of let me take your temp, blood pressure, take more blood, etc.

After all of that, I would then commence my grooming rituals. I am a hoot if nothing else! I'd get my bath in with the Juniper Breeze that my dear friend Lucy Williams had given me. Such meticulous care would I employ as I bathed then dressed up for the day in my Solange lingerie from Lane Bryant...the silky stuff...not sleazy but very classic and colorful. Like me! Everyone else was walking around their in wrinkled cotton wear with their behind's hanging out. I would at least put two on one with my behind hanging out and then I'd have another one on like a robe. What would it look for me to be walking around with my big behind exposed! Not me. Not happening Captain! As Doctor Smith would say "Indeed."

Oh go ahead! I'm an only child let's not forget and I like to play...so if I've got to be here for about 1/12th of my yearly life, every other month or so, I might as well enjoy this hospital which has become my private suite at the Beth.

Finally, I was about to put the pedal to the metal, there it was. My one challenge I believed I might fail in...the timed walking at a brisk pace.

Walking Out My Faith

Jessie once again wanted to know how I was feeling. He wanted to know if I felt I was up to the task at hand. I was a bit unsure and hesitated in my response. Eventually, I thought and steadied myself to get started. Once the test began there could be no restart. There would be no leaning against any walls. It would be walking in the middle. Like being in the flow of traffic without any breaks. No shoulder to pull over to. He had his monitoring everything on ready at my call. The hospital was a buzz all around me paying me no attention whatsoever. I thought to myself, isn't this just grand? Here I am about to run (walk) well it was akin to running for me...and no one was paying any attention. Indeed! I was too through! I'll show them!

Deep breath. Yeah right...not too deep! Then, I chucked to myself and signaled to Jessie to begin. He asked, are you ready? I nodded in the affirmative and silently prayed "Lord if you will" and I was off left right, left right, left right, left right, left right, reasonably long strides, focused not looking at Jessie…just doing the left right, left right, left right, left right, turn, do not stop, left right, don't fall, left right, crap, this is getting tiring, go ahead the Voice said, keep it up, go ahead, left right, long deep breath, left right, left, right, I can do this, thank you Lord, left right, left right, left right, looking at Jessie, I point to my wrist, he tells me I've been walking for about a minute. What?! God help me! The Voice says remember your steps vision. Yes, I do. That is the dream/vision I've always had in my mind's eye of my ascending this great flight of stairs without any hesitation and each step up was steeper than the next and I realized as I ascended I was not out of breath at all. When I saw that reminder from the Voice it was on! And, heard in my head the cheering of those who were awaiting me in the dream/vision who were saying that they knew I would make it and to just come on they were waiting for me! It was all in colors of golden rose brilliant bright and magnificent lights and I was adorned in golden white tinged with sepia rose! Before I knew it…I heard Jessie saying okay stop, stop, stop, Nellie you can stop now! I was dazed; I was completely unconscious of each step I was taking in this realm. I had walked by faith and not by sight, the Lord had walked with me every step of the way…and I had made it because He willed it to be so.

Where is it that you fear walking to today? Fear not, God is with you. He will walk you into your next victory and the ones after that too! Just ask me…I'll tell you so!

There's a thousand more pages I can write about my journey walking by faith and the Lord having carried me when I could go no longer. You've seen the "Footprints In the Sand" picture and read the poem…it's true my friend, surely that has been the all of us at some point in time.

As the Lord would have it I had passed all of the tests to be submitted to the developers of the device. They reviewed the data without knowing whether I was a male or female or what socio-economic station I came from, no ethnicity was labeled or any other criteria that would go to identify or define me as whomever I was. In this instance I truly was just a number.

So the data was sent and placed into a doohickey I guess and the verdict came back. I had won the lottery lock stock and barrel! Bless the name of the Lord! I was randomly selected to receive every option available within the clinical trial. The device, the repair or replacement of any necessary valves and the follow-up treatment that was extensive. The clinical trial was slated for completion in 5 years. Remember this is 2002. That means that I would be involved with this endeavor until 2007.

Getting It Together

Time is of the essence, it's getting to November, a meeting has to be scheduled with my entire family to "discuss" this procedure. There are major risk factors involved here. This is not something that is routinely done. This is a trial. There will be physicians on site in the operating room at the time of the procedure to be there for the cardiothoracic surgeons who will perform the procedure.

However, those physicians and scientists will not be permitted to perform any of the actual surgical procedure. My Cardiothoracic surgeon speaks with my family and myself showing us the device and demonstrating with a device that shows the size of my heart, the size of a basketball. Yes, you read that correctly. Our hearts are supposed to be the size of our fist. Not mine. My friend and former co-worker Pheon, said Nellie I always knew you had a big heart, now it's been proven scientifically. Imagine that!

The surgeon went on at length as to how the device had been designed and created to passively reduce the size of my greatly enlarged heart. He also explained that the mesh netting would become a permanent part of my heart.

We would discuss the matter extensively in this meeting. My decision held firm even after hearing that the procedure could result in death. Once we all understood and agreed that I had made my decision with a sound mind and an understanding of the scope of the procedure and without any coercion then the next step in the process was for me to get my affairs in order.

My daughter was a minor. My next stop was to meet with my attorneys to complete my Last Will and Testament, Living Will, Health Care Power of Attorney, as well as designate someone to have my Power of Attorney for any other matters that could come up should I not be in a condition to handle my affairs on my own.

Having worked in law firms throughout my career especially in Wills, Estates & Trusts, I knew the importance of these documents being put in place. I also had to provide the hospital with proof that these matters had been executed properly.

These are valid as well as challenging aspects in a person's healthcare agenda they are essential to peace of mind. Often time we are left to attend to these matters at the last moment for ourselves or loved ones. And, more likely than not, many of us never even speak of these family matters until perhaps a tragedy strikes without warning. My advice to anyone whether they are single, married, divorced and the like is to put these affairs in order. It's imperative that you handle your affairs before they are required to be handled by someone else who does not know what your desires are should there be unexpected end of life decisions.

These matters were all formalized. There was just one other something left to do, which I did by myself. I drove to my local funeral parlor and met with the manager and made my arrangements for my funeral should there be a need. I explained my situation and she marveled at my strength. I told her I didn't know if I had strength or not that this was something I had to do because my daughter was not yet an adult and should this be my end, I didn't want to labor her with these decisions.

So I spent the next two hours with her making the coffin selection along with all of the other matters that go into planning for the end of one's life. I provided my life insurance policy information, made the necessary assignments for monetary disbursements. You name it I got it done.

Now that those affairs had been put in order. There was the push to have the procedure performed. I started to back pedal a bit here. They wanted to do the surgery immediately. We met again, this time to sign all of the consent forms. It seemed as if I was signing my life away.

I wanted to hold off a little bit. Thanksgiving was to be in a little over a week. The physicians explained to me that once you'd been selected to have the procedure then it had to be performed within two weeks. I pressed saying I wanted to be able to enjoy what could perhaps be my last Thanksgiving. The medical team met and discussed and came back with a modified plan for me. I could have my Thanksgiving, I'd have to come to the hospital the day after and take care of a few remaining preliminary forms that needed to be signed. My scheduled date for the procedure was set for Monday, December 2nd, 2002 at 7:00 am. I was given a strict list of what to do and what not to do before arriving that morning.

Enjoying Thanksgiving with my friend Valerie and her Mom and family was great for me. My family was not available for me to have Thanksgiving with. So once again, my friends stood in to be my family. I'd always wanted to wear my hair platinum. So guess what? You guessed correctly I wore my very long platinum wig for Thanksgiving it was very distracting and gave me something to talk and think about besides the procedure!

That wig was stunning to say the least!

I spent the whole Thanksgiving with Valerie and her family and I even spent the night, too. Valerie was to drop me off at the hospital so I would be able to sign my last documents. It was early morning that I needed to be there and Valerie is a very early riser and got me there on time. Traffic was quite heavy. I bid her farewell and told her I would talk with her later. She said no way Nellie Wosu, I'm going up there with you. I said no Val, that's not necessary. She insisted, I said no. She looked at me crazy and said Nellie go inside and wait for me, I'm going to park the car. I looked at her like what's wrong with you. She didn't back down so I did and simply said okay. Gee whiz I thought what's the big deal? I can go home by myself. Valerie parked the car and came into the hospital and we went into a section of the hospital that is not easily found. This section of the hospital reminded me of the corporations I was accustomed to working in; very elegantly appointed, dark sultry colors beautiful woods, very rich and opulent.

It was there I met my other coordinator, the Physician's Assistant she worked with the cardiothoracic surgeon. She was a young African American woman who was extremely competent and confident in her demeanor. She went over the final need to know info and sign here, sign there, sign everywhere. Valerie sat quietly watching.

Occasionally, Valerie would look over at me. I managed a smile or two. This mess was getting deep. Was there no turning back? My coordinator sensed my apprehension and she took a look at me and pushed the paper work back and asked me what I was feeling? I said I was unsure. She reassured me she'd be there through every step of the procedure. I hadn't been made aware of that. That seemed to give me some type of comfort. I thought that was a good thing to have someone there for me another woman who perhaps would understand what it was all about. She too had children so she knew my concerns. Then we went on signing papers or rather I went on signing more papers. And, then there was the one last one to be signed. Valerie still watching I recall tilted her head and narrowed her eyes. Something had shifted in the room. My coordinator looked at me, squared her shoulders and she had changed somehow in an instant, she was my blood relative. She was still the consummate professional she spoke in an even tone, saying this is the consent for you to sign to give us permission to stop your heart. Time stood still for an eternity. What? I hear Valerie somewhere in the distance saying "oh Nellie, oh Nellie!" I'm frozen. I can't speak until the words fall out of my mouth rather loudly, "you mean you're going to 'Dead me?!'"

Somehow everything had changed before the blink could occur. I protested you're not going to stop my heart. No one told me that I went on rapidly. Oh no, I wasn't aware of that! How could I have missed that part? My coordinator could see I was quite upset. She explained the reasons why it was required and what the process would be like. There was no way getting around doing without same. All of her explanations, of course, were valid. I understood. But still 'dead me'. I thought to myself how else could the procedure be performed? What is going on here with you Anita? The Voice was back in my head again. I don't need to hear this now. Thank you! If you're going to trust Me, then trust me. Have I ever led you wrong? No, You most certainly have not. Anita, I'm here to keep you and prepare you for greater things in your new life. I sat back considered and remembered my Mother saying to me what the Lord had told her about being in Newark Beth Israel Medical Center. That that was the place she would receive her healing. Could her healing be for me I wondered? The Lord would have to let me know because I sure didn't know anything anymore. Valerie was still quietly watching with tears streaming down her face. I steeled myself and straighten my back and reached for the consent form and pen. Then resolutely so, I signed my name, 'Nellie A. Wosu,' I said silently within my heart, in the name of Jesus according to your will not mine. I put the pen down and pushed the paper back in my coordinator's direction. Deed done. If you're going to trust anyone, trust God. His word does not return to Him void. *(Though He slay me yet will I trust Him.) Job 13:15*

So I'm ready, I'm set. Just a few hours more to go. I'm in a T-minus counting state of mind. Valerie brings me home wishes me well I thank her for being there. That's why I decided that she had insisted on being there. God already knew what awaited me upstairs in those chambers. I needed family with me. My blood wasn't there, but my blood was there. At times, those of us who have family or very limited family in close proximity will have to rely upon the family of friendship to assist you in matters concerning your heart from a mind, body, spirit perspective.

I don't know of anyone else other than Valerie, who would have been able to stand there in the gap with and for me while I sat and received that report. With emotion running rampant all through me there was no place to run and hide I was completely undone and exposed. Valerie took the hit for me, she absorbed the shock and the pain for me. That's why the Lord had her to be there with me in that time, she was made for a time such as that in our collective lives. I will love her forever for being insistent on going that extra mile with me by faith.

Hours are beginning to move swiftly. I'm home alone with my thoughts of days gone by. I see everything in amazing color. I hear in Dolby sound the echoes of my life. I cry, I laugh, I wish, I pray, I believe, everything is going to be alright. Mommy shows me in my mind's eye the mustard seed key chain she always carried when I was a very little girl. I see Uncle Fred, my favorite person in the world, he's passed on now. I hear him say 'Neta, you're a young woman, live your life.' I'm done. They all rush around me to comfort me. I hear them all conversations of my life with my family nearly four decades of sound bites play in my head, images run across the optical lens and landscape of my mind's eye. I have always been blessed beyond measure. If God be for me who can be against me?

Tracy arrives on Sunday, we laugh and talk. I'm not listening there's a robot inside of me responding. It's not me. I'm not talking too much. Anyone who knows me at all, knows I can talk baby! So me being quiet is something to behold. Someone else is here with me I sense I'm being covered.

Before I made the decision to have this procedure, I took a survey of many people I've known for years and years and some folks I had recently met. I told them all about the procedure and what it would entail, etc., etc. I asked what they thought. I also let them know I wasn't asking what I should do; I just wanted to know their thoughts. This was in case I had missed something I had not considered. My friend's responses were overwhelmingly focused on Summer, my prognosis and everything in between. These thoughts came into my head flooding me at once this Sunday, December 1, 2002. As you can guess, I never slept that night for some reason not sure why.

This is getting difficult for me to write now. I see it all like it was yesterday. I know the story, I know what comes next. I've been there, told my story to thousands of people in various venues. It never ceases to have an impact upon me. When the Lord does the miraculous for you in due season you'll know that you've been marked by Him. You've been set aside as His own. I am His own. What occurred to me within the next twenty-four hours of my life is irreversible and I wouldn't take nothing for my journey. I don't believe I'd go back to before if I could. No, this is better for all that has happened I am the better for it.

Our God is faithful and worthy of praise at any moment. As the drill sergeant says to us drop and give me fifty or a hundred. So, too, the Lord can say to me drop and give me praise a hundred fold over, and I am compelled to do just that until I breathe no more. I've seen the Lord. I've touched the hem of His garment. I've been the woman at the well, I've been the woman with the issue of blood for more than a year I had a full menstrual cycle every day, one of my cardiac professionals said I was like Job, I agreed and then later wished I'd never agreed to that. But, then I re-read Job and I thought to myself, I'll run on and see what my end result is going to look like. I'm glad I did!

I've lost it all in one form or another; my homes, my cars, my money, my friends, my significant other, my husband, and even for a time, my most beloved daughter. And, what I didn't lose I gave it up freely. There is one thing, however that I've never lost or gave up freely and that is my faith in God. I've gained much and He has recovered it all to me. Everything I have received back, all of it because I believe in Him. One drop of favor from God will carry you through several lifetimes.

We arrive at the hospital they're waiting for us. There's a problem getting my earring out of my ear. Blasted stud, when Tracy and I practically remove my ear, I throw the bedeviled earring in the garbage. It's time to go in now. Tracy looks at me and I look at her. There's no one to sit with her through this ordeal. Our uncle didn't want to come and sit with her while I underwent the procedure. He told her he was not my father. I was concerned for her this could take too long. It was to be a very long surgery anyway. She said she would be okay. We hug say a prayer and she walks with me until we arrive at double doors and we're commanded by a big red sign like a traffic sign to **STOP!** The sign clearly states that only those having the procedure can proceed further. That would be me, Anita.

We cry. We linger. Okay, I'll go, I said. I swallow. I pull back, square my shoulders and I see the stairs again. I ascend the stairs as I push through the doors never to look back again.

There are places in your life that will require you to travel for a time with a companion. And, then all of a sudden, that's where a fork in the road will appear and you must journey the remaining miles without your physical companion. That was clearly evident when the sign said STOP. Only the one who was being taken to another level could go, that one was me. I didn't go through those doors alone, I came through with a Host of Power and unmatched Love. God walked through those doors with me, He had His Son, Jesus there too, and Jesus already had the Holy Spirit inside of me, to be the Keeper of Me, Anita. I was in great Company. How could I not be kept? For God was with me…always in all ways.

The Device

This is an illustration of the type of Device which was fitted to my heart to passively reduce its size.

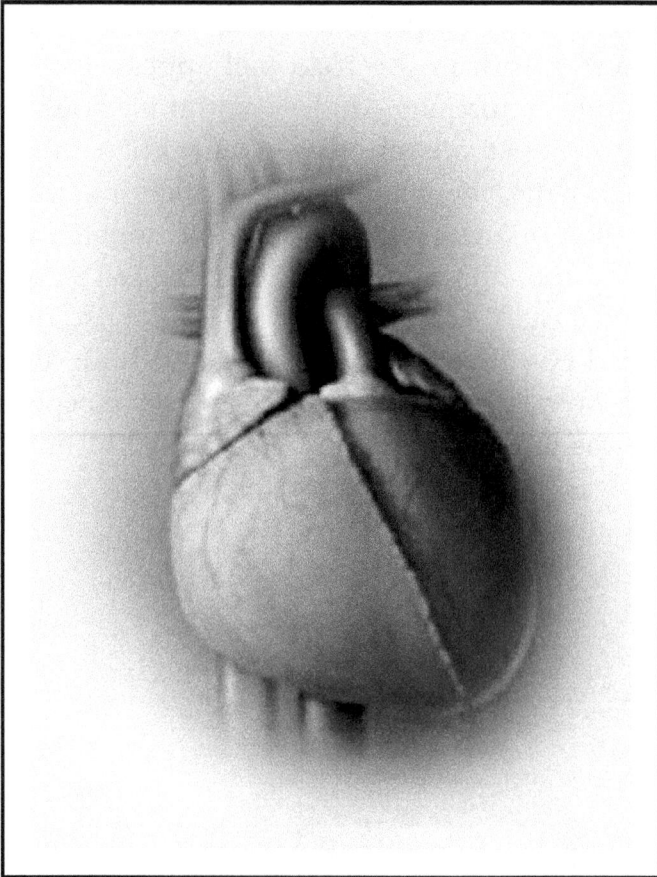

Acorn CorCap Support Device

An Angel of Mercy in the Form of a Nurse

At some point in time, I'm not sure what day, I'm awakened. It is late at night on 3rd shift. I'm not in a typical room. This room looks weird. It's basically all glass and there's a station setup in the glass doorway. A nurse is busy checking and rechecking things. I've got machines all around me on four sides. I've also got the alien in my mouth and down my throat. I can barely move. I'm stiffer than a board. I'm alive. Thank you Jesus! I must have made it through the surgery ok. This doesn't look like heaven. There'd be no sickness there. So I'm still Earth bound. Okay, that's good.

Then my angel nurse arrives. I can barely move like I said. They've got me locked down tighter than Fort Knox. I'm feeling kinda crazy. I'm also dry as a bone parched like I've been baking somewhere. I can't turn my head at all. There seems to be stuff sticking out of my neck. Central line is what it is.

My angel nurse is a God send. She's pleasant and has the most beautiful accent. It's either Irish or Scottish I believe. She's so kind she asks me if I'd like to sit up a bit. I blink once for yes. I can't speak I learn. That alien thing in me. What is that for I wonder. She gives me the run down on what happened and what's now happening and what will happen in the next several, including info about removing the alien. But for now, I'm going to keep it. Whoopee!

She asks if I'd like to have my back washed I blink rapidly. Oh the gift of water! How it refreshes the soul of one parched dry lady. I now know what the Earth feels like in a drought and also what the earth feels like when the sky gives freely of the water within her clouds. I am at once restored by His living waters brought by my angel nurse. I almost pass out with sheer joy. How long had I been under? It wasn't long till I was out again for the count. Fade to black. Eyes open again to much movement 1st shift busy, busy, and busier. Now I've got the whole team running in. I have no eye glasses to see anything. I'm so near-sighted. I can see up close but need my glasses for distance. I'm more alert now. Still holding on to my alien friend in my throat. When are they going to remove this thing I wondered? Checking, checking, checking, everyone is working me over with a fine tooth comb. Oh yeah, clinical trial patient, I hear them whisper stuff then they move away out of earshot. I see I have a television up high on the wall. Humph nice I guess.

He Shows Himself

I look up at the television. Squinting I try to focus my eyes to something on the television. What's that on the TV or actually what's that IN the TV? I tilt my head, trying to adjust myself to see better. The television is a bit far away but I'm seeing clearly there is something in the television. It's as plain as the day. I look over my head. I don't see any lines in this room. Like I said it's a glass room. There are no connecting or intersecting lines in this room. What are those lines? I follow the center lines which is the larger of the three sets of intersecting lines. The center lines are in perfect alignment with me and are poised directly in the line of my incision.

The lines below are very similar to the ones I saw clearly in my television without any other lines of demarcation in the room for those lines to be appearing within my television:

The only conclusion I came to was that He was showing Himself to me to let me know He was there with me just as He said He would be. He never leaves us nor forsakes us.

When folks would come to visit me I'd show them the crosses in the television. No one could see them. My Priest had come to visit me. I told him about the crosses. He looked to see them. He said he couldn't see them. I tried to tell him how to turn his head, etc. I said they're there. He said he believed me. Later during our conversation, he turned around and looked back up at the television and stared a very long time saying nothing.

Afterwards, a friend of a friend, a very spiritual woman named Eula, came to visit me in the hospital, I told her about my crosses, she let me know that they were not there for anyone except me. They were not to be seen by anyone other than myself so I stopped telling folk about them. The crosses remained there watching over me. No matter how I moved the center cross was poised dead center within my incision it never lost its position. The television was never turned on at any time while I stayed in that room, I made sure of that.

I get stronger and soon was placed in a step-down unit that was somewhat Feng Shui in its holistic approach; there was aromatherapy in the room. Lavender was constantly being circulated within my room. The room looked like a very beautiful suite, with the exception that it had a hospital bed. I was given one hour body massages daily as well as a full therapeutic touch healing session.

The added benefit of this clinical trial was that I was exposed to something new to me. Guided imagery. An absolutely awesome and powerful experience. One of the main focuses of this procedure was to enhance the overall wellbeing of the patient from a mind, body, spirit perspective. I was to listen to the Guided Imagery tape two hours every day without fail. The guided imagery was done by Belleruth Naperstek. She has a most unique and distinctive voice, which is comforting and evokes much emotion as you listen to her speak throughout the tape she describes many different aspects of what you've just come through and will go through in the coming times ahead this coupled with the deep rich sound of her voice heightens the experience of guided imagery. I listened to the Cardiac ICU and Rehab tape continually for months on end. This treatment was used to accelerate healing, reduce pain and depression, and motivate exercise and healthy new habits, while cultivating optimism and patience with the recovery process.

Soon I'm ready to return home to a house with no one in it but me. So much begins to happen it's difficult to put it all in writing. Just know that the Lord had a ram in the bush for me by the name of Lucy Williams. After having been sent home with all of my instructions, I was told I had to change my dressings twice daily. I was hesitant and feeling all alone and sorry for myself too. I didn't want to be all by myself. Lucy called one day and said she had been laid off. Then, she said wait a minute Nellie, who is there with you? Me, myself and I was my response. She chuckled and said now I know why I got laid off. Give me till tomorrow, I'll come and stay with you and accompany you to your first medical appointment. And, Lucy did just that, too! Good friends are worth their weight. I have some incredible friends!

Here is where I going to attempt to get this part out in rapid succession because this just simply sends me over the edge every time even to this day.

What the Difference a Day Makes

Everything is going well. My first visit receives a marvelous status according to Dr. Goldstein, my cardiothoracic surgeon. I'm doing everything correctly. I have a date for my follow-up appointment. Good! I'm about two weeks post-surgery. Sniff what's that I smell? Every now and again I get a whiff of something foul smelling. I check myself. Is it me? I thought it might be. I've been told I can't shower or tub bath for four months. Nothing must enter into the incision. I check myself no, I'm good. I'm not stinking. I tell my home health aide,

Patria, she checks me out. She doesn't smell me. Okay. But still there's that faint whiff of something foul smelling in my head or nostrils.

By Friday, I'm in excruciating pain can't inhale or exhale without searing pain. My wonderful neighbor Chris is at the ready again. We call the ambulance for assistance. The firemen arrive, the paramedics shortly thereafter. I explain what has happened to me. They don't know what I'm talking about. The CorCap What Device? Just please take me to Newark Beth Israel Medical Center. Sorry, we can't do that. That's too far away. We must take you to the nearest hospital which is in Jersey City. There was a hospital closer to me. However, they were not a trauma center and that's where I was taken. I won't go into all of the details but here's the gist of it. I'm kept all night in the ER am given some very strong pain medication and sent on my merry way back home. I'm feeling better. By Monday it's gotten worse again. My ex-husband's friend takes me to the hospital in Newark. I go to the heart failure clinic and am seen just about immediately. I recant everything that has happened. I get the look. Repeat that again. I did. Okay. They check me extensively. They have me wait in the waiting room. Come back in please more checking. Nellie we're going to admit you. Okay. My daughter had arrived home from college so she's there. I ask someone to call and let her know what has transpired. I've been here since about eight in the morning it's now later in the afternoon.

My cardiologist, Dr. Zucker tells me he's going to let me go into his private office while I wait for my room upstairs to be ready. Not the examining one. His office. I smile, gee thanks Doctor Zucker! Dr. Zucker's dad later comes in to speak with me. He was such a kind and gentle man. I didn't have much air in me to hold a conversation because the pain was so excruciating. Dr. Zucker's dad said to me that I was going to be just fine. He reassured me of this and held my hand and looked at me intently. He said something which wasn't too audible to me and he smiled and said not to worry. My coordinator Jessie was not there he was away. I had been assigned another coordinator. He was very nice too. He took me to my room. I was weak beyond measure. I needed to go to the restroom. My coordinator waited patiently for me. Then I appeared. He steadied me and led me to sit down as I was about to take a dive. I had no energy to assist myself. He helped me and then he paused looking into my bra which was a very soft front hook type of bra which was required after open-heart surgery. My bra had filled with grey pus inflammation and it was just gushing out of me! Lord have mercy on me! Jesus what is this I screamed in my head? My new coordinator held up my bra and asked me what I wanted to do with this, I looked at it and all I could see was the very tiny red blessed cloth sticking out through all of that gunk. That cloth had been given to my mother by her mother, Nellie. I had it pinned in my bra. When I saw that blessed cloth somehow I knew I would be alright. I told my coordinator to just throw it away.

It wasn't clear what had happened to me. There appeared to be no reason for this. Something had gone dreadfully wrong. But what? No one knew.

The next day, Summer, her father, Pernell, my friend Karen and her fiancé, Joe were there with me. I couldn't speak, too much pain ripping through my chest. What was wrong? Lord what have I done? No answer.

Chika, Summer's father, told her to give me some Jell-O. My hands were useless they shook and trembled. Summer fed me the Jell-O, the red kind, my favorite. I managed a smile. I could tell by the look on their faces they were concerned. To me it seemed they were covering up something. Summer was to return back to school the next day. Pernell came to visit me. The doctors and nurses seemed to come in at the same time, too. What is this I wondered? I looked at them. I couldn't speak for myself. Oh God. I can't speak for myself. I heard the Voice say this:

..., "My grace is sufficient for you, for My strength is made perfect in weakness." 2 Corinthians 12:9

They came to tell me that they couldn't do anything for me any further on that unit. I would have to be moved to the unit where I would have more dedicated care. They were going to put me into a coma to save my life. I sank back and protested silently and visibly crying. Pernell right by my side stood there comforting me. Me looking up at him telling him, pleading with my eyes trying to say I don't want to go. I want to stay here with you. He understood he said "Neet, you have to go. It will be alright." I didn't want to be placed in a coma. My unit clerk came and said to me "oh Lady Wosu, I'm so sorry I've never seen you this sick." The truth was I'd never been this sick in my life. I was dead as a door knob. Someone injected something and fade to black.

Then I feel something, something like cold cement being pushed through my head trying to think. Something is moving but what. It's hard to push a thought can't get it through to my brain to connect. I know something but what I don't know. Trying hard to think. Sludge in my brain can't push through the cold cement. What am I supposed to do? I'm pressed I can't move my body. Somewhere in the deep recesses of whatever was left of me realized something was happening and that I was being transported somewhere. I tried to pray I think.

The verses below have become my cornerstone; they are where I have parked myself and have remained immovable. I know these verses were written with me in mind:

Psalm 118:17-18

I shall not die, but live,
And declare the works of the LORD.
The LORD has chastened me severely,
But He has not given me over to death.

I couldn't seemingly formulate a prayer in my frozen state, therefore, somehow, I managed to think 'ditto'. Fade to black yet again.

After years of going through this in my head I truly believe this is when I was in the coma and they were taking me to the operating room.

Whatever may be going on in our lives there is Scripture that provides truth and a healing balm for us. You have seen that in my writing here. When I could find no solace in my own understanding for whatever challenges I was traversing through, I did find something in the Holy Bible to help ease the pain of isolation in my situation. Reading the Word of God brings us closer to Him every time.

Psalm 38:1-11

Prayer in Time of Chastening

A Psalm of David. To bring to remembrance.

O LORD, do not rebuke me in Your wrath,
Nor chasten me in Your hot displeasure!
For Your arrows pierce me deeply,
And Your hand presses me down.

There is no soundness in my flesh
Because of Your anger,
Nor any health in my bones
Because of my sin.
For my iniquities have gone over my head;
Like a heavy burden they are too heavy for me.
My wounds are foul and festering
Because of my foolishness.

I am troubled, I am bowed down greatly;
I go mourning all the day long.
For my loins are full of inflammation,
And there is no soundness in my flesh

I am feeble and severely broken;
I groan because of the turmoil of my heart.

Lord, all my desire is before You;
And my sighing is not hidden from You.
My heart pants, my strength fails me;
As for the light of my eyes, it also has gone from me.

My loved ones and my friends stand aloof from my plague,
And my relatives stand afar off.

The next thing I know is someone is pulling on my big toe. I jerk my foot as I wake up looking to see who is messing with me! It's them!!! Yay!!!

Tracy, Karen, her Mom, Miss Irene and Pernell. Pernell is still there right by my side rubbing my head. The look on his face was all filled with emotion. Several attempts had been made to get me off of the ventilator to no avail. There seemed to be a problem for me in sustaining breathing on my own for 45 minutes without interruption. Pernell was most concerned about this. Everyone was told that I would have to do the work. I had been through so much ordeal they knew I was in a terribly weakened state. My nurse said she would be back at 5:00 am to get me off of the vent. I said okay by nodding my head. That endeavor was a the testing of my fortitude and a complete ordeal if nothing else. The vent tricks you into thinking you are breathing on your own. However, that is not the case. Pernell said he would come to visit the next morning and bring me some pineapple juice and oranges. He said he would help me get off of the vent. I smiled.

95

One failed attempt after another I couldn't get off the vent by myself. I grew weary and the nurse explained to me in no uncertain terms that if I didn't get off of the vent soon, I'd be a vegetable. My eyes grew wide. Vegetable? I liked them but I certainly didn't want to be one of them! I tried my best to sustain my own breathing only to be told I had stopped and the machine had taken over again. It's okay when you're unconscious being conscious and on the vent just doesn't' work. I had to refocus and try harder. I asked the Holy Spirit what must I do to get off of this dastardly contraption. I heard this *"Inhale Jesus, Exhale Love"* so that is what I did every time I took a breath, I inhaled Jesus and exhaled Love. By doing this I was off of the machine after sustaining breathing on my own for 45 minutes!!! Go Jesus!!!

We must press our way if we want something out of our challenging experiences beyond the lesser expectation of where ever the challenging situation is coming from in our lives. I've said it over and over again. The situations that arise within our life are not for us. I believe they are for others to watch and see how to navigate through difficult waters. So that when their time comes, they will have a point of reference to go by. Watching my mother battle with catastrophic illnesses of epilepsy and later heart disease, which went misdiagnosed for years; caused me to become keenly aware of what faith in action looked like. I saw her turn it all over to the Lord.

My faith was bolstered by watching her endure insurmountable odds. Sure, there were times she would through up her hands, but she would also clasp them together in prayer and ask for strength.

If you're in need of strength in this very moment as you read, then you have it. It is as simple as asking God in His Son Jesus' name, believing you have been granted what you've asked for, you shall receive. You may not see the manifestation immediately, but I believe that once you believe and receive, it's just a matter of time until you see that request in the natural realm. You must first see it in the spirit realm. That's what faith if all about. Your faith must persevere in times of trial!

Look toward this scriptural truth that the Lord's Servant, David penned, in one of his may trials:

Psalm 40: 1-8

I waited patiently for the LORD;
And He inclined to me,
And heard my cry.
He also brought me up out of a horrible pit,
Out of the miry clay,
And set my feet upon a rock,
And established my steps.
He has put a new song in my mouth—
Praise to our God;
Many will see it and fear,
And will trust in the LORD.

Blessed is that man who makes the LORD his trust,
And does not respect the proud, nor such as turn aside to lies.
Many, O LORD my God, are Your wonderful works
Which You have done;

And Your thoughts toward us
Cannot be recounted to You in order;
If I would declare and speak of them,
They are more than can be numbered.

Sacrifice and offering You did not desire;
My ears You have opened.
Burnt offering and sin offering You did not require.
Then I said, "Behold, I come;
In the scroll of the book it is written of me.
I delight to do Your will, O my God,
And Your law is within my heart."

Utilizing the time to ask the Holy Spirit what I must do to become unencumbered with that wicked device and doing exactly what He had instructed, I was free from that old alien thing down my throat. That thing is long! So that's not all of it. When it is removed, everything appears to be alright for a few moments and minutes.

Then suddenly without warning, thar she blows! Get out of the way!! Every ounce of fluid erupts with a vengeful force out of your face and you're trembling like a leaf on a tree in December. So embarrassed. Nurses are great! They smile and take it in stride. My nurse said she was happy for me. I was on my way once again! I was free! Praise the Lord Hallelujah I was free! No more chains were holding me! Another page had been turned for me by my persevering in times of trial.

I waited in anticipation for Pernell all day long. No Pernell. Pernell always kept his word. Where was he I wondered? The day went by no show. The next day still no show. I thought maybe he had to go back to work. I tried calling him no answer. Long story when Pernell had left that evening prior to my getting off the vent. He went back to the house and came undone. He was in the local hospital after seeing me in that condition, it was too much for him to bear. I learned this two weeks later when his relative called me. When he got out of the hospital he came to see me immediately. My hospital stay lasted two months. I went in to the hospital in December 2002 and came out about February of the next year, 2003. I would be home under lock and key for the next several months. I was sick and tired. My incision was healing well. My sternum and incision was handled very differently this time. My diabetes was the reason all hell broke loose after my initial successful surgery. I developed a diabetic infection. Therefore, to avoid the risk of a repeat performance, I believe I was not wrapped up with the wire after the second procedure. My body had to heal on its own. The wire had caused the excruciating soaring pain as I breathed in and out. I've always known diabetes to be a very wicked disease. Should you ever have such take, extra care and caution to treat and manage your disease at all times. It can make the difference in whether you live or die, again.

Psalm 116:1-19

Thanksgiving for Deliverance from Death

I love the LORD, because He has heard
My voice and my supplications.
Because He has inclined His ear to me,
Therefore I will call upon Him as long as I live.

The pains of death surrounded me,
And the pangs of Sheol laid hold of me;
I found trouble and sorrow.
Then I called upon the name of the LORD:
"O LORD, I implore You, deliver my soul!"

Gracious is the LORD, and righteous;
Yes, our God is merciful.
The LORD preserves the simple;
I was brought low, and He saved me.
Return to your rest, O my soul,
For the LORD has dealt bountifully with you.

For You have delivered my soul from death,
My eyes from tears,
And my feet from falling.
I will walk before the LORD
In the land of the living.
I believed, therefore I spoke,
"I am greatly afflicted."

THE KEEPER OF ME

I said in my haste,
"All men are liars."

What shall I render to the LORD
For all His benefits toward me?
I will take up the cup of salvation,
And call upon the name of the LORD.
I will pay my vows to the LORD
Now in the presence of all His people.

Precious in the sight of the LORD
Is the death of His saints.

O LORD, truly I am Your servant;
I am Your servant, the son of Your maidservant;
You have loosed my bonds.
I will offer to You the sacrifice of thanksgiving,
And will call upon the name of the LORD.

I will pay my vows to the LORD
Now in the presence of all His people,
In the courts of the LORD's house,
In the midst of you, O Jerusalem.

Praise the LORD!

8 THE RELOCATION

Finally, I'm back at home after two months or so of being in the hospital. My dear friend, Adriane accompanies me to my first second visit to see my cardiothoracic surgeon. He checks my incision. Adriane is standing behind him quietly observing as she always does. She looks intently. Adriane has been a medical professional for decades. She has hundreds of nurses reporting to her. She looks at me and gives me the thumbs up sign and nods her head. I think really! She nods again in her unassuming manner. I nod back. Dr. Goldstein is looking intently he checks everything and makes his decree that I'm healing up nicely. He's proud of my ability to keep everything proper in the cleaning and dressing of my incision. Remember, I'm wide open, no wires or anything, I'm healing naturally. He says some more doctor stuff to me, tells me to get dressed and he's then about to exit the examination room. He stops dead in his tracks and with one hand on the door knob he begins to twist the knob then he looks back at me, shakes his head, looks at me with those really dark eyes he has and says to me, "it was not your time, it just was not your time." He stares hard and marvels at me for a moment or two still shaking his head back and forth. Adriane looks at me, I'm done. I just stare and nod my head and say thank you Doctor Goldstein. Thank you Lord.

Mark 5:34
And He said to her, "Daughter, your faith has made you well. Go in peace, and be healed of your affliction."

There's much more that will happen to me in the next several months to my health. For a time, the texture of my skin on my abdomen became as leather. My stomach felt as stiff as a leather belt. My legs turned deep red and were inflamed with heat. I also had some type of pooling of water underneath the skin. It was all quite distressing. I wondered when it would end. I rested in the fact that I was still here.

I was on IV antibiotics and oral antibiotics for four months. I dragged myself up in the middle of the night to administer two packs of antibiotics. Levaquin was one of those antibiotics. That's some rough stuff! I made it through by the grace of God. And, yes, I'm still at home by myself, but you know by now, I wasn't at home alone at all.

During this time, I was no longer able to stand the smell of food, I lost my appetite. Seriously, when I attempted to eat my meals which were prepared by Patria, my home health aide, I would gag and have to pull back from the table. Her cooking was great, so was Carol Harrison Arnold's food. Carol would have her cook prepare meals for me and bring them to me. When you're in need, the mercies unfold at every turn to assist you in getting to your brighter tomorrow. Mine was nearing the corner I was about to turn.

Hold on, not too fast, young lady. You have another test to pass. I do. Yes, you do. Suddenly, for some out of the blue reason, I lose the ability to do the left right, left right. Yep, you're right here with me. I can't stand on my own.

Equilibrium out of whack. My legs become too week to hold me up. It had something to do with that pooling of water. So in comes a physical therapist to help me re-learn to walk! I'm glad this passed after a period of times. I had begun to revert to being on all fours to get through my house. God only knew what I endured. I didn't say a word. I was still here. So with that I tried albeit at a pace of cold molasses I did what my therapist told me to do daily to strengthen my legs. It worked, even after all of that loss of strength. I attempted to rock my high heels when I was able to return to church.

Slowly but surely I began to rally. I looked incredibly different. Funny I saw myself looking the same. Everyone barely recognized me. I lost a tremendous amount of weight. The heart was pumping more efficiently. So much fluid had come off of me. I was now a skinny chick! Hmmm, it felt really strange to wear a size 12 verses my size 24. All of a sudden I had an elongated neck. I looked like ET! For real I did. I didn't like the way I looked. To me I looked really weird. My skin was different in textures and tones. But hey like I've said, I was still here, a very good thing to me. So I dealt with it and moved on.

An opportunity came to me shortly after I got home to go to a wedding in Las Vegas. I decided to go. The wedding was to be held in June. I made plans to go. When the time arrived I was reluctant to go. Even up to hours before my flight I was still hemming and hawing about whether I was or was not going. My daughter the logical and practical one said Mom come on now, you've already paid go and have fun. I looked at her thinking to myself, it's you buddy who wants to go and have fun with me being away eight days and seven nights! Yep, I can see it now! Of course, she flat out denied any such thinking. Teenagers, they are a lot like us in retrospect!

I go on my trip and I flip! Vegas is the place for me! No, not the casinos that was the least of what I was interested in. For some reason, I felt I had arrived in my rightful place. It spoke to me, it was my Father's place. The sunshine which warmed me from the inside out beckoned to my weary spirit. When I phoned home Summer could tell something had changed in me. And, it actually had. I was renewed, reinvented, all at once restoration occurred.

Somehow or another, within the last hours of my trip I make a mad dash to buy a condominium in a gated community. Yep, I sure did! I must have been affected by the sunshine at noontime. I was soon to be on my way to a new life with my relocation to Vegas within mere months.

The reasons I thought I was going to Las Vegas to live were totally unfounded during my time there. I would come to meet angels named Cynthia and Kim, they were beautiful women of God who were sisters and they had three lovely children who became like my own to me. Then, I met the golden aura angel in the form of Percilla. These women who were strangers to me, were no strangers to me. They were sent into my path to help keep me in that desert. They fed me and stood by me during my time there. We laughed, loved, went to church, went out to eat, we shopped for furniture, clothing, hair, everything! We even went for drives all over Vegas. Las Vegas is a huge city. I saw Dollar Stores larger than some super markets. In fact, whatever you wanted and if you could name it, you could purchase it in the dollar store, even meat!

Percilla was battling her own form of catastrophic illness. She was on oxygen 24/7. She had Scarcoidosis. All three of these amazing women stood with me as my health plummeted out of the blue on day. I flat lined and was pronounced dead. You see I'm here, don't you? That was in 2004. I wouldn't take anything for my journey.

I've met the devil face to face on many occasions. His job has been to take me out. I'm not going anywhere but where the Lord leads me. So, I've called tech on the practices of the wiles of the enemy. Let me tell you this, if you faint not, you will rise in victory for His glory and to the benefit of many, even up to and including yourself. So be encouraged. If God brought you to it He most certainly will bring you through it.

This I know is certain if the enemy could have killed me it would have been done already. God is the Keeper of Me. I have no life apart from Him. There is no life for me to desire apart from Him. He is the breath that I take. He is the water I drink. God is my all in all. Call it religious call it what you want I call it by faith and He is faithful to keep His word. I believe the report and the word of the Lord. Try Him and see for yourself what He'll do for me, He'll surely do for you too, He is no respecter of person. He loves His children all the same. No partiality will you find in the One who gives beyond measure. Give Him your heart and watch Him teach you how to soar with eagles. Darling, I'm beginning to soar.

From the time I released my faith I made the decision to let it all go, and I got up and left everything I knew to be real and true, gave everything away that I could, and more. I went across the this great nation to a place where I knew nothing or no one and He kept me there.

I didn't get to buy that condo, but look at God, I was able to obtain a condo in an exclusive part of Vegas in a gated community with marble baths, sight unseen, one phone call and I had it. Favor, unmerited favor He pours out upon us. And, get to this. Those new digs were in the same community where I was going to purchase my condo. Look at God! Right where I was trying to land, He took me up and placed me there with no effort required on my part other than to believe. Do you believe?

My story is not unique. There are countless stories out here happening every minute greater than this one. Yours is next. Believe it for it is so! Trust Him as Joel Osteen says, He'll take you to places you've never dreamed of. And, according to Bishop T. D. Jakes, Get ready, get ready, get ready!

And the best of all is the word of truth in advice from Pastor Rhedrick, my Pastor, "Trust God more and yourself less." I tell you if we would simply do this there would be a monumental shift in the situations we go through on a daily basis.

I'm going to stop here for now. I'm spent. I'm moved beyond compare, I never cease to realize that God is truly the Keeper of me and you too. I love you tremendously and you may think you don't even know me. I don't have to know you. I know the Keeper of You, therefore I know you my brothers and sisters.

One note here, angels come to be with us for only a brief period of time. My lovely angels of Evangelist Moody, Cynthia, Percilla and Lucy have left these shores moving on up higher, they have received their greater reward for job well done! Lucy and Cynthia both left as a result of heart disease. Percilla had her double lung transplant and did well for many years. My mentor, Evangelist Moody, left as a result of CHF Stage IV just like me. She walked me through this journey from before the diagnosis. She saw the hand of the Lord work in my ministry and life. She gave all she had for me to tell you to seek the Keeper of You. Don't waste another moment waiting to find Him. He's found you now you go in and find Him and enter into relationship, it will be the best relationship that you'll ever experience in your new life! You'll never regret the sacrifice if you praise God with your whole heart and soul. He promises more because He owns the cattle on a thousand hills, He sent His Son so that you would be able to live. Your living is not valid until you do as Matthew 6:33 says. I'll not include that scripture…look it up for yourself, I believe it will be the beginning of your new life. Live for Him and Him alone!

He keeps me in perfect peace even when the challenges of this life nearly catapult me into the abyss of darkness. Oh yes, it happens. I know, if I'm there, so is He who keeps me.

I involve myself with an assortment of endeavors to assist me in my continual walk in wellness. Sharing my lessons of faith that I've learned with much laughing out loud encourages my heart. I like to help. I hope I've helped you see why your heart matters to Him and to me, too!

I want to tell you so much more, I'm full beyond description. I'm just here for you in mind, body and spirit believing that you're well ... yet again.

Chapters 9 through the Message from my heart were written a while ago. He showed me the end. I believed and still believe. Today is December 22, 2012. I believe there is but One God for us all. I believe in Father, Son and Holy Ghost.

I also believe in free will which was given to us by God. I condemn no one for praying to who they believe they should. I do such so why shouldn't you?

This book is for God's people the all of us. This book is expressly for you, the one holding it in your hands. I too, am no respecter of person. I try daily to be more like my Father. I love you all the same friend or foe. I simply love.

On December 2, 2012, I celebrated my first decade of new life since the procedure. Faith without works is dead. Work your faith and come alive!

9 NEW LIFE

Romans 6:4
Therefore we were buried with Him through baptism into death, that just as Christ was raised from the dead by the glory of the Father, even so we also should walk in newness of life.

Having come through many trials and tribulations for the past 13 years I learned that not only is seeing believing, but believing is seeing that what I could only see as a negative thing in my life was actually the very thing that would catapult me into new life, which was the promise made to me by God right from the very beginning of this magnificent journey. The journey that was to become my tragedy had become my triumph to living like never before. Yes, of course, there are still challenges, twists and turns, but one thing I've learned and know for sure is; if the Lord brought me through hell, death and destruction, He'll do it again for me and you as well.

You may wonder when the new life was promised because it didn't ever appear that it had been promised, but it had.

Here's a scripture that foretold of my new life before it was told to me:

James 5:14
Is anyone among you sick? Let him call for the elders of the church, and let them pray over him, anointing him with oil in the name of the Lord.

The article below was written in December 2006.

The device has made a significant improvement in the quality of my life. The device did not receive approval by the FDA for use in the United States. To the best of my knowledge the trial official closed on or about November 2009. I was interviewed by Bloomberg reporter Avram Goldstein on December 12th, 2006. I have highlighted my section of the report in **bold black italics.**

Acorn Device Shouldn't Be Approved, U.S. Panel Says (Update3)

By Avram Goldstein

Dec. 15 (Bloomberg) -- Acorn Cardiovascular Inc.'s ``heart sock" device shouldn't win U.S. approval because data from clinical trials weren't conclusive, government advisers voted.

The mesh device, designed to keep failing hearts from losing pumping power, wasn't shown to be safe and effective, a committee hearing an appeal by closely held Acorn ruled today. The Food and Drug Administration had twice denied approval for the St. Paul, Minnesota-based company.

Representatives of heart-device makers jammed the hearing in Gaithersburg, Maryland. Acorn argued that a trial with 300 patients showed its device might help heart-failure patients. About 550,000 Americans are diagnosed with the condition each year. Acorn said its investors include Johnson & Johnson, the world's biggest maker of medical devices; Credit Suisse; and Piper Jaffray & Co.

``I have implanted 10 of these devices, and I implore that the panel approve this," said Mercedes K.C. Dullum, a heart surgeon with the Cleveland Clinic in Weston, Florida, in testimony to the panel.

Advisory panel recommendations, while not binding, usually are followed by FDA officials. The committee voted 3-1 against recommending approval.

``This has been agonizing because we are extremely sympathetic to the investigators," said panel member Warren Laskey, a cardiologist at the University of New Mexico in Albequerque who opposed approval. ``We're bending over backwards to try to find a reason to help patients who fall into this niche, but we can't look away from the safety signal."

The agency said it should have a decision in about 45 days. Today's meeting was only the second time a company has used an appeals process created by Congress in 1997 to resolve scientific disputes over FDA rulings. Most companies work out such differences through negotiation.

``Sometimes when you're first, it's painful," said Acorn vice president Steven Anderson in an interview. ``It's not easy to come up with novel therapies." The CorCap received European approval in 2000.

Acorn has raised $80 million to develop its device since the company's 1996 founding, he said. Acorn Chief Executive Officer Richard Lunsford said in an interview after the meeting that he would confer with the company's investors, who have indicated interest in funding a trial that will satisfy the FDA. The company also is developing a way to implant the CorCap without opening the chest, he said.

Enlarged Hearts

Patients with heart failure often develop enlarged hearts as scar tissue builds up. The bigger the heart gets, the less efficiently it pumps oxygen-carrying blood around the body, leaving patients gasping for air and exhausted from everyday activities. As many as half of patients with advanced heart failure are dead within five years of diagnosis, Acorn said.

Researchers supporting Acorn said its CorCap device decreases pressure in the ventricles, the two large lower chambers of the heart, and reduces stress in the walls of the heart while allowing tissue to repair itself in a process known as ``reverse remodeling.'' In some cases, Acorn said, heart size decreased.

Lunsford in a Dec. 13 interview said today's meeting might help device makers learn more about how the FDA uses statistical measures to evaluate devices for treating heart failure.

``The entire heart-failure specialty is looking to try to understand what's the best way to configure heart-failure trials, which are challenging to structure,'' Lunsford said.

Warnings on Data

Acorn repeatedly ignored warnings about its statistical methods and provided data that was ``not interpretable'' and didn't address agency safety concerns, FDA officials said today. The agency's stance dovetails with the recommendation of a 2005 panel, that panel's chairman told the appeal committee today.

``In the end, the panel felt there was an absence of a reasonable assurance of safety,'' said the 2005 panel chairman, Harvard associate professor William Maisel. ``There's a lot of missing data.'' A third of control-group patients got better without CorCap, Maisel said.

Some patients who have received the polyester mesh CorCap device said it improved their lives. Nellie Wosu, 46, a former technology manager at a New York investment bank now living in Concord, North Carolina, said she met with funeral directors to make her own arrangements before she got a CorCap in 2002.

``I once again have my zest for living,'' she said in a Dec. 12 telephone interview. ``I don't have machines at night pumping all around me. I had asked every doctor I could imagine to help me because there was no hope. Now I expect to live a long, long time.''

Robert Stoddard, 78, a retired geography professor in Lincoln, Nebraska, said things have improved since the CorCap was implanted in May 2005.

``I feel like I've got a new lease on life, and I can't help but think the CorCap is a big factor in it,'' he said in a Dec. 13

telephone interview. Stoddard is again hiking, bicycling and working on his land, albeit more slowly than before, he said.

To contact the reporter on this story: Avram Goldstein in Washington at <u>agoldstein1@bloomberg.net</u> .

Last Updated: December 15, 2006 19:08 EST

Note from The Author, Nellie Anita:

The company in which I was systematically discharged from due to the heinous events of 9-11, in a corporate wide downsizing, was instrumental in assisting me achieve a greater degree of wellness unbeknownst to them.

For you see, that corporation was a contributor to the funding of the device which has helped me live a life beyond surviving with heart disease to thriving beyond compare with the diagnosis and prognosis.

To God be ALL the Glory!

Please read Jeremiah 29:11

10 KNOWING WHAT TRUE LOVE IS

Luke 5:37-38
And no one puts new wine into old wineskins; or else the new wine
will burst the wineskins and be spilled, and the wineskins will be
ruined. But new wine must be put into new wineskins, and both are
preserved.

Is it possible to be able to love a mere man when you've
experienced the greatest love that exists?

I've wondered for long what it would be like to love a man
again. Like any woman, at times, we long for a romantic
love that we can physically touch and share our lives with.

Such were thoughts in my mind, living in Concord, being
in a totally new environment. Everything was different and
difficult, at times, that wasn't always what I was
comfortable with or what I even wanted. Living a life in
and for Christ can at times, at least in my case caused me
to question what had really become important to me.
Romantic life was great, I believed.

I dreamt sweet dreams of him. I smiled to myself at the
thought of the two of us engaged in life. I heard myself
thinking one evening on May 21, 2005 at 8:30 pm...

My dear lovely man, how oft I think of you in still quietness, walls of
white space that become filled with the colors of you.

117

How oft I think of you and me in stillness quietly filling walls of white space with a rainbow of mixed emotion through a hushed embrace and lips afire we never tire of telling of a love that isn't supposed to be between you and me.

How oft I think of you while sitting in my room filled with white space – waiting for you to come to this place and fill it with the colors of you; the combing of two with such grace.

These thoughts lead me to temporary solace. The thoughts and your presence actually would leave me vastly depleted.

Something was evident. I had truly changed in my heart. Something had been removed and something else had been placed in its place. I had a new found sense of belonging and purpose. I no longer desired temporary solace in arms that were at best feeble and incapable of comforting and securing my being.

I had an unquenchable thirst that had developed within me through years of pain, shortness of breath, trial and tribulation, agony, loss, separation, grief, defeat, death, hell, destruction of just about everything I stood for as well as almost losing everyone I ever loved. Can't nobody do me like the Lord. He's my friend beyond the end! He is Alpha and Omega.

But, somehow and somewhere in all of that temporary transition and upheaval there was an overwhelming sense of wellness in mind, body and spirit that buoyed a stirring resurrection within me for something more. I desired true

Love. I desired total freedom. So I let it all go. I always knew then that I was an integral part of True Love. I wasn't an afterthought. I was worth loving. I was valued. What mattered to me, mattered to Love.

I have developed a thirst for breath, for free breathing, flying, soaring beyond the arms of a mere mortal mate. I had found true love by simply accepting new life realizing that I always had belonged to Life. I understand now more than ever Life had always taken care of me and always will. With that revelation knowledge settled in me, I began to be able to love better in my relationships.

I found the ultimate love coming from being in the care and sanctuary of the Creator of Creation inside of me, Nellie Anita. I found the Keeper of Me, my greatest Love of all. I am His, I belong to the King. I am the King's kid. My heart and His heart are inextricably bound.

Acts 17:28
...for in Him we live and move and have our being, as also some of your own poets have said, 'For we are also His offspring.'

My physical heart has been touched by the hands of man, twice. I believe the net that was designed to passively reduce the size of my greatly enlarged heart has caused me to grow closer to Him, not just because of the net, or because I now have an understanding of need; but more importantly it is the total desire on my part to enter into relationship with Him, beyond compare. There's been a total change in me. I desire Christ above all!

No matter what situation you may be going through or will go through in due season, it is my prayer that you will find the Keeper of you, too. And, once you do, please do not hesitate to let Him in and have His way! He'll take you to places you've never even dreamed of. This is His promise to you, yes, you, the one holding this book in your hands.

The Lord has given me the desires of my heart.

He has given me new life!

Your Heart Matters to Him, and to Me, too!

Thank you for sharing my story!

Encourage someone today, including yourself!

###

11 A MESSAGE FROM MY HEART TO YOUR HEART

This work has been a labor of love made up of the various experiences that I've encountered from just before I was diagnosed with heart disease up until the diagnosis round about 1999 was beginning to become clear. It wasn't a truly confirmed diagnosis until mid-2000 or so.

The challenges that I've encountered for more than a decade were not just for me. They were divinely designed that I would be compelled to tell you about matters of the heart from a mind, body, spirit perspective and why your heart matters to Him.

Our Lord is concerned about every situation that occurs to us in our lives. We may not always believe this. However, it is most certainly true. And, the Lord is with us with each and every breath we take from before we appeared here up to and after we are seen no more, here on planet earth.

He simply will not, nor will he ever leave or forsake us in any situation. It is us who often leave Him, and in that too, He's still with us every step of the way.

Therefore, just know that my story is for you, the Reader, to let you know you *"Your heart is the central part of your body and without it, nothing else matters. And, your heart matters to*

Him" This is total and absolute truth. I'm not just speaking about your physical heart, which certainly is central and key in everything in your life. However, your spiritual heart is of the utmost importance in your living your life for His glory and to the benefit of many, even including me. Me you may say?! Yes, me, too, because I truly believe that the state of our hearts impacts our collective heart in the natural realm and plays an essential factor in how we ALL fare in our daily lives.

It's like this, when the Lord breathed the breath of life in man that breath has not ceased, even until this time. That breath links us all beyond time and space. I've had a tremendous amount of time to ponder how we're all a part of the circle of life. We are essential to the health and wellbeing of one another. We are a people who whether we want to be are inextricably bound together in some way, shape form or fashion to the next life we encounter. That's why the heart is the central part of the body. We are the body. We are one connected to the Source of All Life. We cannot be just isolated as on an island unto our self. We are humanity created for His good glory to the benefit of the all of us. The missing link may simply be that we've forgotten that essential truth in living as one people, God's people.

My point is made clear in my being by this: Should there be something unpleasant in your situation that is disturbing to you and I'm somehow in your life (and I am for we are

122

here on Planet Earth together) then if you're sad so am I. True, I may not "feel" it as deeply as you do. However, I feel you and in doing so, I'm a part of your experience. Likewise, on the same hand, if you're rejoicing then I have even more reason to rejoice with you.

I believe, problems come about for humans when we become jaded and cynical, covetous and the like. We've all been given grace and an abundance in love. If we are all soaring what better symmetry in life? Have you ever watched the birds fly high above in the sky? Some fly hither and yon, others sit perched on a branch. Then in an instant something magnificent happens, no sound is heard but for some reason they all begin to come together and fly in a pattern that is breathtakingly beautiful, that is life! When we all come together on one accord it truly is a wondrous sight to behold and to experience with every breath we take and the quickening of our collective heart.

Maybe I'm just someone who believes that we are one from the Only One and that one is not the loneliest number that we'll ever know. For one is united in singleness of purpose for reasons far beyond our limited capacity to understand. But, maybe just maybe, if we're willing to try to see the beauty in becoming one in all of us even as to the uniting of all, we will become one, to the benefit of the all of us, and that is a very good thing and most importantly, for His glory!

Therefore, with that being said, let me restate this for you to ponder in your heart as Mary did when she had been told of the miraculous that was to happen to her. By faith she believed and thus it was so for her. And, aren't we, the all of us, the better for her faith? I choose to believe that we are.

We've been given an opportunity to birth a new spirit in truth and love that our hearts are central to not only every one of us but especially to God, Himself, for He is our Heart and the Keeper of us all as His Only Beloved.

Treasure the moments in your own heart and that in others heart, too. Making sure to safeguard it valiantly with gentleness and ever increasing love and appreciation for your ability to:

Inhale Jesus and exhale Love.

For when you do, where ever I am you're assisting in enabling me to thrive beyond compare.

I truly believe that the only way to total wellness from a mind, body, spirit perspective in matters concerning ones heart, is to let go and let God have His way in one's own life.

Remembering Job,

'Though He slay me, yet will I trust Him.' Job 13:15

Thank you so very much for considering me enough to care for your heart so that not only will I be well in mind, body and spirit but you will be, too!

We belong to and are all One!

ABOUT THE AUTHOR

- Minister Nellie A. Wosu, a New Jersey native, has worked tirelessly on behalf of women battling heart disease as well as those who are at risk of developing heart disease.

- As a National Spokesperson and Champion for WomenHeart, The National Coalition for Women with Heart Disease, Nellie has shared her own testimony of living with the disease.

  Minister Wosu spends her time on projects that encourage and strengthen others. She is an active member of First Missionary Baptist Church, in Concord, NC.

  Nellie also writes for magazines and performs in stage plays that she as well as others has written.

- Nellie resides in Concord, North Carolina.

Your latter will be greater...

"To understand the heart and mind of a person, look not at what he has already achieved, but at what he aspires to do."
~Khalil Gibran

For I know the plans I have for you," declares the LORD, *"plans to prosper you and not to harm you, plans to give you hope and a future.*

Jeremiah 29:11 New International Version (NIV)

Selah.

Selah is thought to infer that one should pause and reflect on what has been said. I ask that you do just that based upon what you've read in this book.

Proverbs 4:7
Wisdom is the principal thing; Therefore get wisdom. And in all your getting, get understanding.